~ praise ~

"As honest as it is witty, Ford's memoir acts as both a meditation on modern love and an ode to family and cinema. More than that, *This Dating Thing* truly is one of the more enjoyable literary experiences I've had in recent years. Simply put: It's that good."
– Luke Ganje, author of *The Beginning and The End*

"Maybe it's the film buff in me, maybe it's the rom-com lover lurking within, maybe it's just my fondness for well-crafted tales—whatever the reason, I was utterly charmed by Ford's memoir. Ford hooked me early on with a classic young-love-gone-nowhere and kept me engaged throughout with his wit and clever film references. It's the perfect book for anybody hoping to laugh with someone else about the absurdity of dating, the struggle of finding love, and the sometimes-difficult task of fitting in." – John Katsanakis, author of *Pomegranate*

"I laughed. I cringed. I was completely swept up in Ford's quest to find true love. The best memoirs not only let you see what the author saw but feel what they felt along the way. *This Dating Thing* will resonate with anyone who remembers longing for more out of life and wondering if they would ever find their own love story worthy of a Hollywood movie. Highly recommended!"
– Anita Casey-Reed, from The Cinema 100 Film Society

The only photo I have from their dating thing is Mom standing on a New Mexico roadside mischievously hurtling a snowball at Dad.

this dating thing

~ a movie buff's memoir ~

todd ford

Todd Ford

ISBN: 9798483995302

Photos from the author's shoeboxes

Cover design by Luke Lageson

~for the women in my life~

Aunt Gwen, Cheryl, Mom,
Trissa, Amanda, & Rachel

~ acknowledgments ~

MANY PEOPLE have assisted me with this book. Much love and thanks to all of you—especially those who appear in these pages. The times we shared have been related here to the best of my memory. I've changed some of your names for various reasons, so only you know who you are.

I'll single out a few:

Karen Van Fossan read my prior book, *See You in the Dark*, and told me over lunch that she mostly skipped the movie reviews but adored the stories about my family and me. That was the moment *The Art of Memoir* entered my life. I bought Mary Karr's wonderful book and began to get ideas.

Rebecca White read my first draft. I was at that point of self-doubt otherwise known as "impostor syndrome" where I wanted to delete the whole damn thing and move on to something else. She encouraged me to keep going.

Carrie Classon started reading one of my drafts, stopped halfway through, and gave me some lessons of her own about the art of memoir that I'll never forget. My structure became simpler, an emphasis on just telling a story became front and center, and two kids who might have been included are not because the book would've needed twice the pages to do them justice. (Maybe I'll write a second memoir someday.) Carrie also influenced me both by her own beautiful memoir *Blue Yarn* and by encouraging me to read the works of Elizabeth Gilbert.

Daniel Engelke read a draft and had many encouraging things to say. He also sat me down in my backyard over beers and said, "I love how this is framed as a letter to your daughters, but if you're going to keep that you better make a few changes." That resulted in a flurry of edits and the loss of two chapters. I've never missed any of those words. My wife asked what those chapters were about. I smiled and said, "You'll never know."

Dear Amanda and Rachel,

You never know what's waiting just around the corner, so if you have something to say, don't wait to say it. Don't delay expressing what's in your heart, like Richard Dreyfuss in Steven Spielberg's Always, *waiting too long to say "I love you" to Holly Hunter, leaving her always wondering. "The love we hold is the only pain that follows us here," Dreyfuss tries to say to her from the Beyond.*

I've spent over five years searching for the words on these pages. I wrote them for both of you. I also wrote them for my mom. When I was 22 and about to head out into the world on my own, she asked me what one thing I most wanted to be remembered for when I left this Earth—a weighty question posed to the young me—but I replied quickly, effortlessly, "I want to write a book." It seemed a natural reply. She, along with her sister, my Aunt Gwen, had instilled in me a love of reading. I knew my answer would please her. And it did.

Sadly, because it took me so long to write this, the second promised book, my mom never had a chance to read it, or any version of it…

~ contents ~

the movies

OOPS!

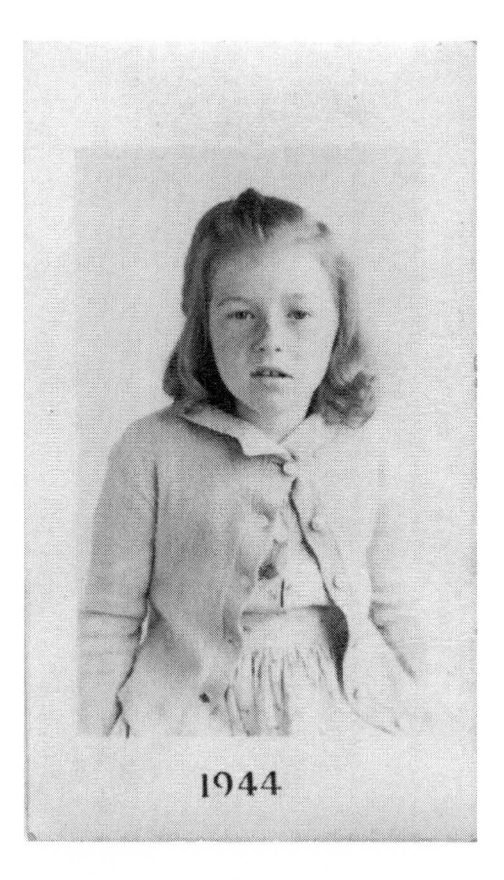

During the service, one slide—of my mom as a 9-year-old girl—appeared and I sobbed as I'd never cried before in my life.

"I DON'T know if you know this, but you were an 'oops!' baby," my sister Cheryl told me as we wandered about Ivy Lawn Memorial Park in Ventura, California. We were searching for the gravesite of our grandparents on Mom's side, Fred and Dorothy Williams, and their youngest daughter, Gwen. Mom had died three days prior at the age of eighty-two. We wanted to bury her ashes along with her daddy, mommy, and sister.

Traipsing toward the shade of one tree after another, we remembered the grave as being near a distinctive tree, although the nature of its distinction escaped us. We'd last been to the cemetery for Aunt Gwen's burial seventeen years ago. But once we located the site, we knew. The tree leaned, dramatically, as if about to topple.

"Dad didn't want kids, but Mom did," Cheryl continued. "They got careless and you came along. Afterwards, they figured may as well have another."

Dad—as the story goes—feared their children would be like his wife and have cerebral palsy. (He had zero understanding of what caused her condition.) I don't believe that account—or it's not the whole story. I think he feared their kids would resemble him: wandering away and selfish.

Despite his fears, I arrived, and not without agony. Mom labored over twenty-four hours for scant profit. I entered the world by cesarean section, tiny, a mere 5 pounds, 10 ¼ ounces, and distressed. When it was Cheryl's turn two years later, the surgeon reached straight for the scalpel.

I met with Cheryl for one day spent wandering about a cemetery and eating Indian cuisine before she took off for a long-planned writer's conference. She's a romance novelist.

So, I had a week alone with memories of Mom as I prepared for her memorial service.

I visited old haunts: my childhood home on Perejo Drive (to glance at the houses of my babysitters and an alto-sax-playing girl of my teens), Dos Pueblos Senior High School (to wander about the deserted campus and jiggle the band room's locked doorknob), and the UCSB campus (to see how it had changed since I'd been a student). My memories of that campus are of a radical place with VWs and bicycles and where the students had recently torched the Bank of America. It now felt Republican with BMWs winking at me right and left—mostly from the Right. I ate salmon and eggs at the Cajun Kitchen Café, twice. I took long walks on "Grandma's Beach." I sat alone with cups of coffee in Mom's suddenly vacant assisted-living apartment. People using walkers asked me three times a day—sometimes the same person three times—"Where's Bev?" I stretched out on her bed admiring her Seattle Opera poster for a production of Gounod's *Roméo et Juliette*—a long-stemmed red rose on a dark green background—and filled the pages of a notebook with blue ink in my shaky printing. (Don't expect to find those words on the following pages. They were for my eyes only, words that led to my burst of tears during her memorial service. Tears I didn't want to display publicly but am happy I did.)

The funeral home sat in the long shadow of one of my favorite places in Santa Barbara, The Arlington Theater. Mom's memorial service was beautiful. The pews filled. The slide show I spent all week trying to make perfect was perfect. And when a microphone was passed around, Mom's friends shared many fond memories. Mom was an unforgettable people person. The stories told were often punctuated by laughter.

The highlight of the service for me, though, was the furthest thing imaginable from laughter. It came when my daughter, Rachel, stood and thanked everyone in attendance for telling so many nice stories about her grandma, so many memories she didn't have and wished she did. We're a family of introverts, but Rachel is the exception. I don't know how she forced those words through her sobs. She spoke for all of us.

"Did I do okay?" she asked me later.

I hugged her. "You did perfect."

As we traveled home a few days after the service, I felt proud. In a sealed letter to Cheryl and me, Mom specified not wanting us to make a big deal out of her death. No obituary, no service; her ashes she wanted scattered in the Sierra Nevada Mountains where our family vacationed in a cabin near Hume Lake. We defied all three of her wishes and instead gave her the send-off she deserved.

After arriving back home in Mandan, North Dakota, I double-clicked my Microsoft Word document containing this memoir. I'd been working on it off and on for four years. I took a deep breath. I wasn't sure how—or how much—what I'd just experienced was going to affect the book, but I knew it would.

As it turned out, Mom's death changed everything.

GOLETA

Before Grandpa Carl, I assume, snapped the photo, Cheryl stepped in between Shelly and me—protecting me from Shelly or, perhaps, Shelly from me.

~an upside-down kiss~

IN 1967, at age five, I was obsessed with *Batman.* When I watched TV, my yellow blankie became a cape and my jammies tights. I'd hear the show's rousing opening theme song and see Batman and Robin running toward me, trying to leap into my living room, "Sock! Pow! Zok!" This was when Batman popped out of the television screen in vivid primary colors *played* by Adam West, long before he lurked in the shadows of a movie theater *acted* by Christian Bale.

Mom hated *Batman.*

"The violence will rot you inside out," she told me.

She forbade me to watch it, her "wholesome boy." (When I watch episodes now, her concern sounds ridiculous. The show is cartoonish and, as I watch the Joker and Batman compete in a surfing contest, I burst out laughing.)

Of course, I rebelled, a determined boy on a mission. Mom taught elementary school as a substitute teacher, and I'd spend hours every weekday at a pushover neighbor's house. Babysitting time included Bat-time. I kept quiet and thought Mom would never find out.

But I must've let something slip (maybe by walking around babbling about Batman and Robin scaling the sides of buildings and good guys punching bad guys' lights out) because Mom arrived early one day and caught me with "WHAP! BIFF! OOOOF!" splashed across the sitter's television screen.

I never watched *Batman* again as a young boy. I also started going to a different babysitter, a fortuitous change, as it turned out. Without being careless and getting caught in the Bat-act, I never would have met the four-year-old daughter of my updated babysitter. She eyed me. I smiled back.

On day one, our lips met, and we discovered how it felt to

kiss. I don't remember any talking, just us hiding in her garage. I remember laughter as we experimented with different kissing angles. Her head steady at twelve o'clock while I rotated mine ever so slightly to one o'clock was our favorite.

The daily fun went on for a while, a week or less, but we soon became carefree, unconcerned with confining our game to the garage. My last memory of her is an upside-down kiss. She hung by her knees on the jungle gym. I sat in the sand below. Her mom watched from the kitchen window.

I've wondered how long the episode might have lasted if we hadn't been reckless or if her mom hadn't been watching. I doubt she remembers me, and I don't recall her name, but I'll never forget her kisses. They had a sweetness that made me think of a peach Grampa Fred plucked from an out-of-reach branch, wiped with his shirt, and handed to me when I was four—a taste I would store away until years later, when I'd meet a young woman named Monica.

IN 1973, my family visited Oklahoma in July to hang out with my Grandpa Carl (Dad's dad). On the third morning, I awoke from a sweaty night's sleep. (My grandparents' house had one air conditioner, hovering over their bed's headboard. One night during the same visit, I sleepwalked and stood upon their bed in direct line of the cold current—totally freaking them out.) I wandered into the living room, which was imbued with a peculiar lack of breakfasty smells. Adults paced about, listening to the radio. I kicked back on the couch and watched. Mom entered the room, spun around twice, and searched out the window.

"Tornado!" she screamed.

I had never experienced a twister, not even a warning or a watch. They're not common in Goleta. Mom had fretted and for several summer visits expressed concern over the house not having a storm cellar. The reality had arrived.

"Where will we hide?" she kept asking anyone who might listen.

Having grown up in Oklahoma and never having been

killed by a storm, obviously, Dad sat and poured milk into his bowl of cereal.

I considered myself a tornado expert. I'd seen *The Wizard of Oz*. I found the development a fun bit of excitement plopped into the middle of our vacation. Ignoring Mom's warning to stay away from windows—she didn't want window frame fragments conking me on the head like Dorothy—I scanned the horizon for dancing, bending, and twisting funnels of mayhem working their way across the landscape lifting cows, houses, and wicked women on bicycles and transporting them to faraway Technicolor lands. I imagined myself carried aloft and flying high through the skies, watching people in rowboats and bathtubs as they drifted by, smiling and waving as if virulent storms happened to them every day. I wished our dog Princess wasn't confined back home in a kennel. She could've been my Toto. (She looked somewhat like Toto. Shortly, I'll properly introduce you to her.) I imagined spending days—or forever—strolling about the Land of Oz with Princess, cavorting with flying monkeys and fighting over apples with talking trees.

A hand grabbed me by the shoulder and hauled me toward the center of the house where I now imagine us huddled, the family of apes from the befuddling beginning of *2001: A Space Odyssey*, afraid to peek outside our cave. The wind howled louder and louder, and the house shook. The wind blew softer and softer. Then quiet.

The adults stirred. We moved toward the windows to peek outside. Shafts of sunlight broke through the clouds, forming a rainbow which brought a melody to my mind. Except for a few broken tree branches littering the street, everything looked normal. Neighbors strolled about looking groggy as if they'd awoken from a nap. Then *they* arrived, one by one—neighborhood kids ready to make the world right again by assembling around Grandpa Carl.

What followed was a candy-munching, story-filled gathering of neighborhood kids circled around my grandparents' back step. The two stories fixed in my memory featured his fingers. An index finger had a fleshy nub where a fingernail used to be.

"Was helping my dad feed pork into a grinder one day while making a batch of sausage and I slipped!" he said.

"*Ahhhh, ewwww*," the kids responded in chorus.

That first finger's next-door middle finger had been sliced top to bottom and had jaggedly semi-mended.

"My dad told me to be careful with his table saw."

Children gasped as he wiggled the finger before pairs of eyes, all as tilted and huge as the twin suns Luke Skywalker contemplates in his most vulnerable moment alone on Tatooine. (I'll tell you more about *Star Wars* later. Luke's reflective moment before embarking on his life's big adventures is my favorite in all of cinema.)

I don't remember most of those kids, because only one mattered. Shelly. I occupied her mind as well. A surviving photo shows her smiling, a bit shorter than me, wearing brown cutoffs flaunting tanned legs and a lacy top exposing her white as snow belly, an Oklahoma lass enjoying summer, anticipating a snowy December. Before Grandpa Carl, I assume, snapped the photo, Cheryl stepped in between Shelly and me—protecting me from Shelly or, perhaps, Shelly from me.

I spent the afternoon glancing at Shelly, losing myself in her lips as red as licked cinnamon candy and dark chocolate hair as she folded and unfolded her hands in her lap while listening to Grandpa Carl. She'd occasionally try to capture me with her emerald eyes and I'd narrowly escape to fumble with *my* hands. (Okay, I don't—and didn't—know the color of her eyes. I avoided them completely. But I do love dark shades of green, and her last name? Green.)

What had happened to me? At five, I smiled and kissed my babysitter's daughter. Six years later, I couldn't look Shelly in the eyes. I found a series of pictures taken at Hume Lake. They show me as a six-year-old hanging out with the cabin owners' granddaughter, my summertime fling, Kendi. We'd hold hands and sneak away to play "house." I could've been a Casanova.

Later, Shelly and I sat on the back porch, slurping root beer floats Grandma Earla Mae (Dad's mom, to me simply "Grandma") prepared for us before conspicuously leaving us alone.

Shelly's nine years exceeded my eleven according to crazy new math.

"You're adorable. Please stay all summer," she told me.

I sat, blushed, smiled. I should've been returning her compliments or better yet beating her to them, but my mouth wouldn't cooperate.

Shelly went home leaving me to spend the rest of the evening daydreaming about the two of us. As she made her exit, she gave me a lingering kiss on the cheek before slipping away. I spent my final evening in Oklahoma composing a love letter. O, my Shelly, you left me with only words to play with! I asked Grandpa Carl to give her the letter, after we hit the road.

"Please, not before!"

I don't know if he ever gave her my letter (maybe he read it and thought better of it), but when I asked him about it a few months later over the phone, he claimed she'd been excited by my note and couldn't wait for me to visit again.

"Grandpa, when you see her, tell her I miss her."

"Do you have something to write with?"

"Yes."

He told me her phone number.

"Why don't you give her a call?"

"I will, Grandpa."

I lied. The notepad and can of pens and pencils sat as far out of reach as Oklahoma.

~*this* boy and his dog~

EVERY SUNDAY night during the late sixties, I'd plead to stay up "one more minute!" Lassie might not forgive me if I didn't wave goodbye to her, but *Lassie* ended past my early bedtime. I'd often have to resort to sneaking out of my room, inching my way to the end of the hall, peeking around the corner at the TV, and seeing the collie of my dreams lift her paw. I'd raise my hand in a reflection of her gesture and retreat, hoping Lassie had seen me.

Mom and Dad helped me forget about Lassie one day by taking Cheryl and me to the Humane Society. We walked from cage to cage looking at one barking dog after another. I wandered off, hearing a faint whine from the cat room. And there she was: a tiny pup, a motley gray-and-black-furred mix of toy poodle and toy dachshund. Too small for a dog cage, she'd been stashed with the kittens. I opened the cage, picked her up, held her, and wanted to never let her go. I named her Princess, after my friend Tommy's cat.

There's never been anybody like *this* boy and his dog. When forced apart, such as during trips to Oklahoma, I'd miss her terribly. Together, we "talked" constantly. I have two etched memories of Princess, the first so deeply it feels as if it's happening right now.

During a late morning with the California coast gloom not yet lifted and the dew on the grass half-evaporated, Dad mows our enormous backyard lawn, United States-shaped if viewed from the sky. He pauses to watch a butterfly take flight ahead of his spinning blades and flutter away to safety over the fence. He stops the mower and boosts himself up. Standing upon a horizontal two-by-four he continues watching until it travels beyond his vision. He returns to the mower, sighs, and pulls the cord to start the blades spinning again.

He's grooming the coast of Maine. I'm bounding about with Princess in Arizona. We're playing our favorite game, "Get the 'nail." I run along the edge of the lawn, stopping to bend over and brush my hands through the blades of grass. Princess chases after me, barking.

Whenever I expose a snail, I freeze and point at the ground and say, "Get the 'nail! Get the 'nail!" I raise the pitch of my voice to increase her excitement. I giggle over my playful snipping of the word "snail."

She rushes over and snaps up her prey. I hear a crunch. She spits it out and looks at me with her tail wagging. Sometimes, I hear the crunch, but nothing comes back out.

"Don't *eeee*-eat it," I say. The tone of my voice makes her butt wiggle.

After Dad works his way around the contours of Florida and the Gulf Coast, Princess and I relocate to North Dakota. (Why did he landscape such a complicated lawn? To guarantee caring for it would be a lengthy distraction?) As he cruises the California coast, headed toward Oregon, we return to Arizona and make use of the freshly cut turf, which makes our hunt too easy. I spot plenty of shiny brown shells under these conditions.

"Get the 'nail! Get the 'nail!!"

Crunch crunch. Spit.

"Get the 'nail!!"

Crunch crunch. Gulp.

The screen door slides open and Mom yells, "Lunch!"

I look at Princess. I'm tired, hungry. She's still game. I say, "One more."

I spot a snail chopped in half by the mower blade.

"Get the—"

She pounces before all the words escape my mouth.

Gulp.

We head inside, and Mom has grilled cheese sandwiches and tomato soup ready at the table. I sit and dig in. She bites a corner off her diagonally cut sandwich half.

"Who were you talking to out there?" she asks.

"Oh, nobody," I answer as Princess and I exchange private

glances.

Years later, after I'd secured my driver's license and a car, Aunt Gwen helped friends exercise their horses on a ranch and Princess and I tagged along, driving separately. When we arrived, I took Princess for a walk. We wandered around the perimeter of the ranch house, having a relaxing time. It was a sweltering day, but there was an abundance of trees and plenty of shade. I let her leash out to full length to let her roam. Suddenly, a dog from the ranch bolted from the darkness beneath a porch and attacked Princess. Princess was meek. The attacker resembled a wolverine, a mass of spit, fury, and tangled fur. I couldn't see Princess trapped beneath the monster with dust flying everywhere. I pulled on the leash, hand-over-hand, and dragged Princess free. She yelped.

I screamed at the attacker as I clutched Princess in my arms. I kicked gravel in the evil dog's face. The ranch owner saw it.

"Leave our dog alone!"

I opened my mouth to protest, but nothing came out. The owner ran toward me. I leaped into my light blue VW Bug, carefully placed Princess in the back seat, and sped away, distancing us from the situation as quickly as possible. I stopped on the shoulder of the road, shaking in the still running car. Princess was whining. Then I smelled it. She'd emptied her bowels all over the back seat.

I hopped in the back to comfort her, oblivious that I was sitting in her mess and checked for wounds. She wasn't injured. There was no blood. She moved without limping. She was frightened.

I sat for hours fuming and daydreaming and scheming about going back to the ranch and killing the dog and its owner, blood and limbs flying everywhere, an orgy of gore worthy of Carson Napier, Edgar Rice Burroughs's fierce Venusian hero. (That author's pulpy books lined my shelves and affected me deeply and, yeah, not always in ways flattering to my young character.)

I've never been one to hold onto anger for long, though, and by the next day I merely settled for never venturing near that ranch ever again.

SOCIALLY SPEAKING, I haven't changed much over the years. I've always been in my comfort zone while around pets. Plunk me in the middle of a social gathering and I wonder:

Are they cat people or dog people?

The answer doesn't matter. I'm equally fond of felines and canines. But if I see no evidence of pet loving, I know I'm in trouble.

I can sit in a yard and stroke a cat's fur or toss a ball for an eager dog for hours. I'll hold entire conversations with them. I'll ask them if they find these people-gatherings as tiring as I do. They do.

I consider this behavior mostly benign. When playing "Get the 'nail!" with Princess, I was happy. Life should be a pursuit of happiness. When it replaces human interaction and conversation, though, it becomes a problem. As a kid, and a teen and a young adult, I epitomized social awkwardness. I've improved. While around my wife's large, extroverted family, I can't squeeze a word in edgewise, but once I maneuver one or two relatives off to the side, talking about something of mutual interest like writing or Vikings football, I settle in.

I can't deal with conflict. When it comes to fight-or-flight, I flee. A movie scene I frequently quote is the "Ballad of Sir Robin" from *Monty Python and the Holy Grail.* Rather than consider myself a coward, I prefer to say I bravely run away.

~teeny tiny briefs~

MY FAMILY hit the road in 1975. The nation was preparing for the bicentennial year and we beat the crowds. I sensed feelings of doing it now or doing it never.

We made a brief pit stop in Oklahoma, but Shelly didn't reappear. Maybe her family was touring the country as well. Seeing her would've been a nice pick-me-up; my final image of Goleta before hitting the road had been of Princess, whining as the kennel doors clanked shut behind me. Dad and Mom had been in a hurry. Nashville and beyond beckoned.

As we entered the state of country music, Dad's spirits took flight. He'd long dreamed of visiting the Grand Ole Opry. While driving, he warbled "When Will I Be Loved?" and "Movin' On."

"I hope Linda's in town," he said.

"Who?" Mom asked.

"Linda. You know, Ronstadt. Merle, too."

"Uh-huh."

"And I'd give anything to see Dolly."

"I bet you would."

The songs and names meant nothing to us kids. As billboards for the city sprouted, we wanted to veer into the campground and walk off our car-queasiness, but not Dad. He made a beeline for the Opry House to buy tickets for the following evening. We all sat in the pickup cab while he went inside the ticket office. After an eternity, he slinked back out of the building and as he walked toward us, his whole demeanor changed. His face turned red. No more singing. He walked with a slouch and his arms kept thrusting downward as if trying to punch the ground. There's a scene in the movie *The Shining* where Jack Nicholson strides through the corridor outside the ballroom and makes the exact same arms-thrusting gesture. I always laugh when I watch it and think of Dad.

"I hate Jack Nicholson! Nobody ever acts the way he does!" he once told me.

Dad slammed into the front seat and punched the steering wheel. "Three weeks! Sold out for three weeks!" he said, his words rushing past us. He drove to the KOA campground, outside the city, and checked in without saying another word.

That evening, dinner around the tiny booth in our camper felt especially cramped. Mom sat facing the window. Dad ate standing up. Both teary-eyed.

"That's that. May as well turn around and go home," he said.

"Don't start," she said.

"Don't you!"

Mom stood, leaned toward a cabinet, and found two Mason jars. She handed them to me.

"You and Cheryl go outside. They should be coming out soon," she said.

We stumbled out of the camper, clinging to the door handle as we stepped out onto our wobbly plastic step stool.

"That's how I feel, Bev! That's how I fu—" Dad's word was cut off by the door closing behind us.

They continued. The heated discussion, incomprehensible, drifted through the open roof vent and spread out across the campground. Nearby families paused and looked toward our camper, over at us with concern, and back to their own affairs. Cheryl and I exchanged glances. Our parents weren't arguers. We'd never heard *this* before. We didn't know what was happening. So, we blocked it out and roamed the campground clutching jars to our chests. (Maybe only I blocked it out. Events like this always seemed to hit Cheryl squarely while I merely received glancing blows.)

Our experience for the evening: chasing and capturing the copious fireflies sparkling in the dusk. We expected the hunt to be challenging, as if trying to catch ordinary flies, and stealthily waved our jars through the air. We soon discovered fireflies are born as if wishing to be caught. They live for bringing joy to kids who are having a horrible evening.

We wanted to play and to forget, and the fun and intoxicating ease of catching the tiny creatures had us laughing and racing about. With our jars filled and shining brightly enough to read by, we sat on a bench.

"I got a million," Cheryl said.

"No, more like thirty-five," I said.

"Shut up."

I had mixed feelings about those tiny creatures. Catching them felt exhilarating, but seeing what I imagined to be frightened looks in their tiny, anthropomorphized eyes filled me with sadness. They were trapped in our jars as Cheryl and I were trapped on this trip in a tiny camper, tempting me to place my jar on the bench and remove the lid.

The location of our camper had become a mystery. Everywhere we looked we saw nothing but trailers, motor homes, and tents, and happy families sitting around campfires chatting, singing, and toasting marshmallows. We followed the road through the campground using our jars as lanterns.

Afraid our parents had left for home without us, we turned a corner and spotted it, our yellow Dodge pickup with bed-length temporary home, the dome light illuminating the interior. Mom sat on the back bumper awaiting our return and when she recognized us in the dark, she let out a full body sigh visible from four campsites away. We went inside, heard Dad already snoring, crawled into the booth, which had been converted into a bed, and lay still until the sound of Mom's slumber reassured us. Then we drifted away.

I awoke in the morning to hear Cheryl crying. I rolled toward her.

"What's the matter?" I asked. She didn't answer.

I noticed she had her jar nestled in her arms. I looked inside and saw stillness. I checked my jar. Same. Apparently, fireflies give joy for only a single night.

I rolled out of bed to use the portable toilet hidden behind a curtain and noticed Mom alone in the bed above the cab. I looked outside, where Dad sat at a picnic table staring into a cup of coffee—a behavioral quirk of despair he passed on to Mom. Before they married, they negotiated one peculiar arrangement: he had to cease smoking and she had to drink coffee. I suspect it was the only thing they discussed and agreed upon. He benefited from the better end of the deal. I never once saw him smoke, while she drank coffee with an occasional grimace for the rest of her life.

I climbed onto the edge of their bed.

"Are we going home now?" I asked Mom.

"No."

Instead, we cut our visit to Nashville short and hit the road, headed east. When we entered Knoxville, Dad exited and pulled to the shoulder.

"Why are you stopping?" Mom asked.

"We have to decide. Do we head to the Dakotas or keep going?" he asked in return.

"You know all I care about is Williamsburg."

"Oh, God. Must we?"

"Tom. Please. Don't."

He put the pickup in drive, re-entered the freeway, and continued east.

DURING THE following two years after arriving back home, Dad became fanatical about new trends. After my lifetime of never seeing him exercise, he lingered in the master bedroom puffing and sweating through morning push-ups, squats, and sit-ups in his underwear—and not just any underwear, but bright red, teeny tiny briefs. I'd see him on the floor sweating before taking his shower, hair on his chest and back, his pot belly, his graying and receding hairline, and how his thing barely stayed out of sight. Cheryl could walk in at any moment! Mom could walk in! It horrified me his wife might see the outline of his… thing. His efforts paid off. The pot belly melted away.

But the effect was short-lived, and he soon found a way to re-pack on the pounds. We were the inaugural family in our cul-de-sac to purchase a microwave oven. After hauling the Amana monstrosity home, attempting to shimmy it from the box before losing patience, cutting it free with a steak knife, and plugging it in, Dad demonstrated how we could bake apples in record time—a mere minute and a half.

He removed a green apple already cored and filled to overflowing with brown sugar from the fridge, ready to go on a paper plate. He lowered the heavy, spring-loaded door and placed the apple in the oven. He released the door and it closed on its own. He pushed a few buttons and the machine whirred.

"HEEERE WE GO!" he said, resembling an infomercial.

(When I recall his words, now, they sound more like "HEEERE'S JOHNNY!")

We'd never had baked apples before, so I'm not sure if the brown, bubbly messes he created were typical, but over the next few weeks, we—well, mostly he—ate a lot of them. He invited neighbors to experience the miracle of instant baked apples. He entertained the idea of going into the instant baked apple business, but soon the fashion wore off. Until we discovered quick popcorn, the fast cup of tea, and the art of bringing leftovers back from the dead, we simply became the house on the block with the least amount of usable kitchen counter space.

As if changing channels still again, Dad switched to color television. He didn't buy one, not exactly. He mail-ordered one through a company called Heathkit. The ads declared, "Announcing the first solid-state color TV you assemble yourself!" as if it were a prize-worthy idea.

Our "television" arrived in several boxes. To Dad's excitement, and everyone else's dismay, the boxes contained a jumble of wires, tubes, screws, and twisted scraps of metal and plastic. The objects giving me hope and promising future enjoyment were the picture tube and the cabinet.

"Do you guys have any idea how much a twenty-five-inch color set costs?" he asked, and continued without waiting for an answer, "I'm sure you don't so I'll tell you. A lot."

Every Saturday morning for weeks, I stared at the corner of the living room—a makeshift workshop—and hoped to see something capable of playing cartoons. Each time, I turned away disappointed and returned to watching Bugs and Elmer in black and white. Making matters worse, the television once "finished" never fully worked. It always had strange bands of indistinct colors running through the picture. Dad didn't—or couldn't—see them, so captivated was he by his accomplishment. (He never *truly* completed it. A few parts left over didn't fit anywhere. He considered them "extra" parts and tossed them into a drawer.)

He talked to us less and less the closer the "television" came to being a semi-television. One day, I walked into the living room to check his progress and saw him mounting the picture tube into the cabinet. From where I stood, I saw his two legs sticking out from beneath the set. He'd been consumed by the TV. It reminded me of the Wicked Witch of the East after Dorothy dropped the house on her. I swear his socked feet curled and disappeared.

I don't remember the moment the project was "finished," the black-and-white set was banished, and the intruder assumed its post in the center of the living room wall. I do remember our old set sitting on the floor of my parents' closet facing the corner. It had been placed in a time-out. A few times, after trying to watch the interloper for a while, I snuck into their room, slid the closet door open a crack, and patted my old pal atop the head.

After Dad's labors, I don't recall him ever once sitting and watching his Heathkit. Always "at work," he spent his days at IBM, but he never talked about what he did there, and I never thought or cared to ask. I knew it had to do with something futuristic and electrical called "computers," assembling them, fixing them if they broke. My one experience of him working on electronics had been our television set. I pictured his desk at work cluttered with "extra" bits and pieces of computers he'd later stash in drawers. I imagined him as not a particularly competent computer whatever-he-was and, given his lack of shoptalk and general grumpiness at home in the evening, not in love with his job either.

Mom was terrified when he came home early from work one day and announced he had been "let go." His income and future retirement prospects had gone *poof*, but he looked oddly relieved.

He increased the intensity of his bedroom floor, semi-naked workout sessions. He washed his cherished Oldsmobile Cutlass daily. He wore shiny silk shirts unbuttoned to his navel. He dangled a gold chain around his neck and experimented with hair dyes and comb-overs. He eventually bought the *Saturday Night Fever* soundtrack album and wore it out. He embodied a walking, talking, dancing cliché—the dad in the movie *Dazed and Confused* who thwarts his son's attempt to throw a keg party. Richard Linklater set his marvelously researched movie in 1976 and Dad found polyester in 1977. Despite his efforts, Dad always lived a bit behind the times.

One detail did separate him from the father in *Dazed and Confused.* Dad never would have prevented a keg party. He would've joined in and smiled at all the girls. Cheryl told me, "When Dad helped me move in during my freshman year in college, he went away for a while, returned, and stocked the fridge with four cases of beer, one for me and each of my roommates."

These behavior swings were all barely noticeable at the time, but they were accumulating in my mind. Eventually, in Dad's increasing absence, I had to mow the lawn and it grew shaggier by the week. All the excitement about instantly hot food dissipated. The television's picture worsened until it stopped working entirely and our small black-and-white set returned atop the otherwise useless Heathkit cabinet. We ate at the coffee table—and even in our bedrooms.

~interchangeable mouthpieces~

I DID more than eat in my bedroom. I spent countless hours in there roaming the jungle with Tarzan during my tweens and teens. As an adult, beyond a vague recollection of *Jungle Tales of Tarzan* being my favorite, I hardly remember those boyish adventure stories. I still have my paperbacks in a box in the basement. I dig around, brush aside cobwebs, and blow away dust. I favor the black-bordered covers with artwork by Neal Adams. On the *Tarzan of the Apes* cover, Jane Porter is fetching as she waits for Tarzan to kill a fierce ape. I give that and *Jungle Tales* a fresh read after forty-two years, looking for clues to my past.

As you know from my parting words to Shelly, I'm most comfortable expressing my romantic feelings in writing. (I'd hone my skills years later.) Tarzan initially contacted Jane Porter using a love letter. He declared, "I want you. I am yours. You are mine." I hope Shelly (or only Grandpa Carl?) found *my* declarations less embarrassing.

But why did I cherish *Jungle Tales*? It's piffle. Well, I *was* a girlfriendless teenager. I'd walk from class to class, always past the dreaded lockers to see one couple after another using the ten-minute break to squeeze in a bit of romance. I once saw the ceramics teacher sneak a quick extra-marital snuggle with a history teacher. At the core of *Jungle Tales* is Tarzan's longing for a mate, and the stories all occur during his teenage years as he watches animals of the jungle enjoy love. The first page describes him sitting upon a low-hanging branch admiring Teeka, a young female ape.

Now, I didn't squat in trees, much, but I identified with gazing upon feminine loveliness. At the time, I fancied myself a photographer. I saved my dozens of favorite photos, including plenty of my high school's drill team, organized in a dark green album, hidden away in the same box as my Edgar Rice Burroughs library.

The album is also dusty, and the stickiness of the pages has released its hold. Pictures slide out onto the floor as I pick it up. I gather them and toss them inside the front cover.

As I flip through the pages, I see lots of photos of Princess and a few of Cheryl, and one of those captures my curiosity—it shows her and the hands of another girl. They're both squeezing sponges into a bucket of soapy water. I turn the page to see a gallery of three photos devoted to my VW Bug, showing the hood, the door, and the roof. The focus is shallow. I'd been playing with the telephoto range of my Soligor 80-210mm zoom lens, maintaining a safe distance. Centered in all three shots is the face of a neighbor girl, the owner of those hands. She's in blue jeans, wearing a white halter top, and has her brown hair in a blue and white bandanna. Anny.

Emotions flow through me now. She was such a sweetheart. If I'd been a different me, she might've spent time inside my car. I laugh at how transparently I spied on her with my long lens. In all three shots, she's focused, carefully washing my car, working a spot on the roof, shining the door handle, and caressing the hood.

All these years later, I sigh and turn the page.

I FOLLOWED in Dad's footsteps and joined the high school band. I played trumpet—truthfully, the instrument I played was his stubby and embarrassing old Navy cornet, which looked pathetic beside my bandmates' long, blaring silver bells. Buzzing against the warm, wet, round surface of my two interchangeable mouthpieces was the only action my lips enjoyed in those days. And those partners experienced paltry practice time. I forever sat third section, second chair.

I had a crush on an alto sax player—Sue, one of Cheryl's semi-acquaintances. She sat first section, second chair, but instead of saying hi I trembled whenever near her, every school day from 10:00 to 10:50. From my chair during band practice, I had an unimpeded view of her music stand and of her long, smoothly shaved legs stretching out beneath it. She often wore shorts. The sheet music on my stand seldom came into focus.

Once, shortly after passing my driver's test, I took Sue and Cheryl to the beach. The sight of Sue walking out of her house toward my car in a bikini, a towel around her waist and sunglasses atop her head, nursing a Coke from a bottle overwhelmed me. I barely remembered how to drive. I stalled the engine while backing away from her house. While stopped at a red light, I stole glimpses of Sue in the rearview mirror, posed in the tiny backseat. I started rolling forward and would've lightly rear-ended the car in front of us if Cheryl hadn't yelled, "Todd! Watch out!"

While at the beach, I spread my towel a short distance away from the two girls and eyed Sue. I didn't speak. I glanced about the sunny seascape—frolicking, chatter, inflatable balls and volleyball nets and sandcastles. Children laughed. Girls applied suntan lotion. And yet, on my towel, I remained.

I imagined Sue to be Jane Porter. I became Tarzan. I stood, clothed in a loincloth, clutched my knife, strode through the sand, and kneeled upon her towel. I took her in my powerful arms and crushed her lips to mine.

Oh Jane, I mean Sue, I want you. I am yours. You are mine.

I imagined her chest heaving. No need for words; our passions provided all the dialogue.

When time came to depart and drive back to Sue's house, my fantasy, unfortunately, ended. The wind was blowing and I failed to gauge its direction. I stood, grabbed my towel, and shook it clean of the sand it had collected. Sue then blurted out the only words she ever spoke to me.

"What the hell are you doing?! God!"

She wiped my sand from her tanned, lotion-shiny body and stomped off. She became Jane from the *Tarzan of the Apes* cover, but she didn't wait for me with breathless anticipation. She spurned me. On the way to my car, she spotted apes—I mean guys my age—with a pickup and nabbed a ride with them. The next time I saw her, she was tongue-kissing the driver, a wide receiver, pressing him against his locker. After I imagined disposing of him in Tarzan-like fashion, I took his place. Our kisses were fierce, but no tongues. I wasn't ready for tongues—not even in my imagination.

Led Zeppelin helped me survive my subsequent Sue-less days. I made tapes and listened to their albums everywhere I went on a bulky cassette player using ungainly headphones. Once, on a band trip to Los Angeles, I packed my Zeppelin gear and plenty of spare batteries. To make room, I ditched socks and underwear. I figured nobody would be close enough to smell me anyway. In the evenings, I ducked into my sleeping bag, always on a rock-hard school gymnasium floor, to re-emerge as Jimmy Page holding a double-neck Gibson. My psychedelically prismatic performances of "Stairway to Heaven" and "Since I've Been Loving You" became legend.

On one such evening, the chaperones gave in and allowed the students to have a dance. The boys camped out on one side of the gym, the girls on the other, leaving the bulk of the basketball court available as a dance floor. I tried to pretend *Hot Streets* by Chicago wasn't blaring—"No Quarter" and "Kashmir" helped—but I watched as Sue danced with one guy after another. I felt certain each of her partners glanced at me and winked.

Then the distraction came. I heard knocking and rattling and looked over toward the double glass doors by the concession area. Locked as well as padlocked from the inside, the doors shook as a dozen guys—high school students? Older?—attempted to break in. I figured they wanted our girls. The chaperones tried to wave them away. They weren't budging. Years later, I would recall them while watching zombies trying to break into a department store in *Dawn of the Dead*. Eventually, I fell asleep. I awoke at dawn, the zombies long gone. Sue sat across the gym, still safe and sound in her sleeping bag, stretching and yawning. I thought, *That's good.*

CHERYL THREW a party at our house for her friends, and I was there too, by default, living there and all. I never went to parties and was irritated because these people were in our house making noise while I wanted to read or watch television. (I laugh when I watch *Back to the Future* and Crispin Glover's George McFly resists asking Lorraine on a date because he'll miss *Science Fiction Theater*.) At one point, I wandered into the kitchen to grab a Coke and a trap sprang.

A frighteningly cute girl seated in the living room in a group of terrifying females beckoned. She found me intriguing, an about-to-be junior, and her big chance to impress by being with an older man. She sent Janie (a girl at the party I could talk to) over to lasso me and pull me out of the kitchen. I eyed Janie's approach, hopeful, but...

"Michelle wants to dance with you," Janie said.

"No!" I turned on my heel and fled.

I retreated to my bedroom, chased by the sounds of what I took to be laughter at my expense. Soon after, Janie knocked at my door. We talked as she twirled about on the chin-up bar in my bedroom door frame.

"Don't worry about her," Janie said.

"I, umm, didn't feel like dancing, that's all," I said.

"You sure have lots of books," she said, looking past me while hanging upside down. "Which is your favorite?"

"Oh, *A Princess of Mars*—no, *Jungle Tales of Tarzan*."

"Those're cool," she said, flipping right side up again.

Why didn't I ask her to dance in the privacy of my bedroom? We could still hear the music, "Shake Your Booty." Or better yet, why didn't I seize my chance to steal my life's second upside-down kiss?

Years later, I ask Cheryl if any of her girlfriends had ever talked about me, fishing for juicy, nostalgic bits about Janie. She comes through.

"I don't recall you being 'on the radar' for any of my friends. I always thought you might have had a thing for Jayne, but while she knew who you were, you weren't 'in her sphere.' She was the epitome of popular girl—volleyball, usherette, maybe drill team. I can't remember."

To Cheryl, she's Jayne. To me, she's always been Janie. It's as if I'd planted a flower bed in my youth. The seed packets bore generic labels such as "Assorted Party Girls," but a few sported specific names. One grew "Shelly" blooms. Another promised a perennial "Jayne." In the fine print, the packets mentioned the flowers would evolve within the shifting soil of my mind until over forty years later, when they'd each become a modern species. Shelly is now a misty vision, all candy lips, wishfully green eyes, and chocolate hair skipping about. And Jayne? She has become something novel. She's evolved in my mind from the unattainable Jayne to the almost kissable Janie. (I swear Cheryl called her Janie, once upon a time.) My "talking to her" involved no more than the few words I've included, scrunched into one encounter in my bedroom doorway.

These girls live in my mind as floral symbols, but they were also real girls. And I was a real boy. I never ventured into their minds, but what went through mine?

I never allowed them to become three-dimensional. I barely allowed them *a* dimension. They were all pairs of shiny, red, hopefully sweet-and-fruity-tasting lips pursing in an imagined alternate universe, but as hormones raged, so came fears. I'd watch kids my age drift in and out of relationships as nonchalantly as trying out different flavors of chewing gum. I couldn't take dating lightly. The moment after a girl might've said "Yes!" to a date, I would've been planning our honeymoon. I don't know how I would have handled the inevitable breakup, but I doubt "nonchalant" would have been an applicable adjective.

Fridays transformed my high school into rock concerts. Student bands, consisting of "loadies" (slang for kids who cut classes and lounged about doing drugs all day) would perform half-hour sets in a concrete amphitheater known as "The Greek" for our lunchtime entertainment. Aerosmith and a less crazy Ted Nugent filled the airwaves and we'd be treated to covers of their latest hits. Van Halen really got me. Sue once remarked, loudly enough for all to overhear, that she considered David Lee Roth "SEXY!"

Why couldn't I have been the loadie surfer dude Jeff

Spicoli, played by Sean Penn in the movie *Fast Times at Ridgemont High*? He floats through high school without a care in the world and everything goes his way. Or I *was* him. He had both arms wrapped around women in bikinis and hung out with rock stars, but only in his dreams. In reality, he had his bedroom door closed and every square inch of wall space covered by pinups.

Friday nights, I'd place Van Halen's debut album on my turntable, throw on my headphones, kick back, close my eyes, and imagine myself on the concrete amphitheater stage during lunch. Everything out of my imaginary pipes from "You Really Got Me" to "Ice Cream Man" had girls swooning and rushing the stage. For the evening, I traded Tarzan for David Lee Roth. A tiny bit of reality drifted in—at least the lead singer of Van Halen isn't completely fictional. As a prancing and glitzy rocker, I would be mobbed by girls, and I wouldn't have to say anything. I'd frolic with chicks for free.

Back in my teenage bedroom, I'd lessen my ambitions and morph into Eddie, playing killer licks. I'd become Alex flailing away at my skins and smiling in the background. Skipping poor Michael Anthony altogether, I'd consign myself to be a roadie lurking in the wings with Eddie yelling at me to crank his amplifier. Inevitably I'd snap back to another Friday night alone in my bedroom rereading *The Chessmen of Mars*, my evening dream interrupted by the sound of a needle sliding and popping back and forth after the fade-out to "On Fire." I'd climb out of my bean bag chair, place the needle back on the cradle, and tuck myself into bed, where I'd close my eyes and once again become Todd. As I fell asleep, Princess would snuggle in with me, my groupie for the night.

~gazing at two suns~

IN 1977, when I was fifteen, Mom dropped me off alone at the curb in front of the Arlington Theater to watch *Star Wars*. The Arlington dates to the silent movie days when it held sneak previews. Chaplin, Lloyd, Pickford, and Garbo would finish work at the studios, drive north to Santa Barbara to watch a movie, and catch a yacht for San Simeon all with such regularity you could set your watch by their arrivals and departures. The theater is a spectacular structure adorned with a towering spire. The interior is painted to give one the impression of being in the presence of the Santa Barbara Mission with its unique twin bell tower architecture. The seats are plush red faux velvet. The ceiling is blue with clouds and stars twinkle as the lights dim. (It meant everything to me to take my daughters and son-in-law there and show them the place.)

Star Wars. The movie everyone said everyone had to see. The line to buy tickets was short, about twenty deep. Once I had ticket in hand, though, I realized not only did everyone have to see it, but everyone *was* seeing it. I followed the ticket-holder line to the right. People in the front of the line had long since settled in. They reclined on blankets littered with McDonald's hamburger wrappers. A few played guitars. I continued to wander around the corner of the building, down the side, across the rear lined with dumpsters, and back up the other side. I took my place in line at the left front corner of the building. I saw Mom still sitting in her car looking worried. I waved. She waved back and drove away.

I craved science fiction—John Carter of Mars, Carson Napier of Venus—pulpy stuff, tales of muscular Earth men transported to worlds populated by towering, four-armed green warriors bearing swords and the babes they fought over. (A few years later, the golden bikini Princess Leia wears in *Return of the Jedi* would be inspired by Dejah Thoris's garments from the Martian novels of Edgar Rice Burroughs.) I had zero interest in all the Robert Heinlein hippy crap or Isaac Asimov hard sci-fi my few geeky friends devoured during *their* lonely evenings spent in *their* bean bag chairs. So, I felt skeptical. I'd seen commercials on television and this *Star Wars* thing looked like *2001: A Space Odyssey* mixed with a western. God, I hated westerns. I could tolerate Kubrick's movie except for the apes and the boring old bedroom, but John Wayne? *Gag.*

Inside the theater, I settled into one of the few remaining seats on the far right-hand side pressed against a guitar-case-lined wall painted to resemble the Mission courtyard. I slumped in my seat and stared at the ceiling as its stars twinkled on one by one. Soon the words "A long time ago in a galaxy far, far away…" filled the screen.

On that screen, I saw a hero remarkably different from Tarzan. Luke Skywalker wasn't muscular and confident. He didn't know how to "get it on" with the ladies like David Lee Roth, either. Skinny, uncertain, and solitary, he stood alone gazing at two suns with the music swelling, imagining his possible futures—and I knew I loved him. The moment he was me was when the princess rewarded him with merely a quick kiss, a peck on the cheek, before swinging with him through the Death Star. I hoped I'd one day find my own Force and the confidence to trust it and go with it. The ending left his future so tantalizingly open. Anything became possible for young Luke—and for me.

In 2015, *The Force Awakens* brought me to tears at the moment when Luke turns to face Rey atop a remote island mountain. His loneliness and isolation affected me. He looked old. I was getting old. It'd been so long since we'd last shared adventures. And I love those dusty old Jedi books Luke has lined up on a shelf deep inside the trunk of an ancient tree of knowledge in *The Last Jedi.* Same as my Tarzan books for me, they're remembrances of his past—although luckily for me, unlike for Luke, mine truly were page-turners worth reopening.

A new hope entered my world in 1977. Those feelings arose out of a long slumber in late 2015 and I began writing this memoir.

In 1977, I walked out of the theater in a daze and hopped into Mom's car. I didn't say anything all the way home. I replayed every scene in my head. I wondered what lived between the covers of those science fiction novels my friends read. I started watching westerns with John Wayne and loved them.

~introverts trying to converse~

MOM STRUGGLED with my shyness and she blamed it on my face, horrified by my relentless acne. My skin didn't resemble a pepperoni pizza. Black olive and sausage more aptly described it. She caught me one afternoon licking the peanut butter and jelly knife.

"Put it in the sink! You're only feeding your pimples!" she said.

She took my sandwich and bit into it.

"Mom!"

"You want girls to like you, don't you?"

I made countless visits to the dermatologist, where he'd zap my zits with liquid nitrogen. I can still feel the sting. I scrubbed my face with an assortment of funny-looking and stranger smelling bars of soap. The worst popped out of the box orange and transparent. It burned and merely gave me redder, shinier, angrier zits.

At one point, the rock band, The Knack, swung through town. Mom bought two tickets and handed them to me. I cringed. Other than "My Sharona," they promised a monotonous evening. I squirmed because I knew her plan. I still had Janie on my mind, and Mom knew it.

Mom and I stood face-to-face, one on each side of the dining room table. She arranged the tickets, aligned on a place mat. She opened the White Pages before me and circled Janie's phone number in red ink. I stared at the phone. She stared at me. I plucked the receiver from the cradle and fumbled with it for a few moments, put it back, snatched the tickets, and retreated to my bedroom. I took Cheryl to the concert.

That night, the three of us—Mom, Cheryl, and I—sat scattered about the living room with plates of food in our laps. I avoided conversation. Mom led it. Cheryl tried to stay out of it.

"I want you to call her," Mom said to me.

I said nothing and stared at my Swiss steak.

"Todd?"

"She'll say no," I said while scraping away flavorless tomato sauce.

"Do you have any friends he can ask?" she said, turning toward Cheryl.

"Umm…"

Mom studied her for a moment and turned her gaze to her own plate.

"If you don't start asking girls, Todd, I'm going to start asking for you. Brenda's daughter Kimberly doesn't date either and Brenda's worried about her, too. She locks herself in her room and reads like you do. You should ask her out."

I gasped. Kimberly was super quiet and gorgeous. Oh God, there's nothing as awkward as two introverts trying to converse.

Mom said something under her breath—about wanting grandkids, I've imagined. (The times she's sounded the most excited were when I called her to tell her my two daughters had been born. When I called her desk at work after my first daughter Amanda's birth, someone else answered. I tried to leave a message but the woman on the line said, "No! Hang on. She's running this way.")

The discussion about my lack of dating ended—for the day. The next day and the next and the next, the topic returned. In her passive-aggressive way, she kept me on the teetering edge of a mother-arranged hookup until… something.

Something became her placing a phone in my hand, pointing at her open address book, and making me call Kimberly to ask if she'd ride with us to church youth group on Thursday. Yes, *that* innocuous.

I dialed. I trembled and it took three tries. A soft voice answered.

Gulp. Throat-clearing sounds. "Hi…" Pause to catch my breath. *Near choking sounds.* "Hi, uh, Kimberly."

Gasping sounds from Kimberly. "Y…yes." *Gulp.*

"Um…"

"Uh…"

"Would you…um…"

Mom listened until she couldn't take it any longer, took the phone from me, and asked to speak with Brenda.

Dad couldn't fathom me either. I recall a wordless exchange between the two of us. One evening after dinner, Cheryl leaned over the bathroom sink splashing cold water on her mouth, crying. I sat at the foot of my bed. Dad stood in the hall between us, looking at Cheryl.

"I burned my lips on…on…on my pizza," Cheryl said, moaning.

Without missing a beat, he replied, "Someday, all the boys are going to be giving your lips plenty to burn about."

He turned and looked at me. Instead of speaking, he shrugged and walked away. He realized, no matter what words he conjured, I would never be causing a female rush on lip salve.

I don't know which one most affected me: Mom, pleading I'd have a girlfriend if I tried, or Dad, with his resignation that I'd never be setting the ladies' lips on fire, but I feared Dad's intuition was more accurate. And that fear placed me in such a deep funk I wished my bean bag chair would turn into a portal. If I sat in it hard enough while clutching *A Princess of Mars* tightly enough, I'd pass right through it and land on another planet.

AS I reflect on this story and think about Kimberly, our fumbling phone conversation becomes poignant. She acted as nervous as I did, the call prearranged by our moms, part of a scheme. After Mom snatched the phone, Brenda joined her on the other end of the line so quickly I imagine their kitchen scene mirrored ours. Sadly, I liked Kimberly. I think she liked me. Under less stressful circumstances—and a few years later—something might have developed.

She reminds me of Anny. If, instead of spying, I'd helped Anny wash my car, who knows? She might have spent at least a few dates in the passenger seat. If I'd asked Kimberly about her favorite books, she might've blushed as I did when Janie asked me about mine. We might have talked. Who knows?

Dad's dismissive glance also suggests his big move had already been decided. He'd given up on me—and on us. A short time later, a matter of weeks in my memory, on Christmas morning 1977, Mom uncharacteristically remained in bed and Dad sat Cheryl and me in the dining room. The sun poured in through the opened curtains. He was backlit and I couldn't make out his expressions.

"There's no easy way to say this," he said, "so I'll just say it. I told your mom I want a divorce."

"Why?" Cheryl asked, her cheeks already streaked with tears.

I said nothing. I walked back to my bed and pulled the covers over my head.

~done with adulting~

AFTER THEIR separation (the divorce process would drag on for a year), I went out with Dad to a movie and Cheryl went out with Mom. I wasn't a movie nut yet and Cheryl never has been. We had no awareness. They were just movies. So, our choices mocked us.

(Cheryl and I did have one movie tradition. We'd see each new James Bond adventure on opening weekend. Much like my preference for Adam West's silly Batman, I've always had my softest spot for Roger Moore's Bond. My favorites were always the goofiest, like *Octopussy* and *Moonraker*. Curiously, once Cheryl and I lived far apart, I lost interest in James Bond movies. I'm not sure if it was due to missing Roger Moore or missing my movie companion—probably both. I've always found Daniel Craig too serious for my tastes. I loved laughing together while driving home.)

Dad and I saw Steven Spielberg's *1941*. It's a huge, occasionally funny slapstick comedy with the Japanese forces in WWII attacking the California Coast. It includes the destruction of a coastal amusement park eliciting a mournful gasp of "Hollywood!" from a young Japanese sailor who fears they have obliterated the place of his dreams. It's one of Spielberg's extravagant refusals to grow up. It has a general who ducks into a movie theater, escaping the realities of war for a few hours to weep while watching *Dumbo*.

Dad had a blast. Done with adulting, he'd ditched the family, the mortgage, everything. He had taken flight: a true Spielberg hero. One short year prior, we'd watched Richard Dreyfuss in *Close Encounters of the Third Kind*. Dreyfuss plays a man named Roy who is going through a spectacular midlife crisis. His boss fires him. He drags his wife out to experience something "monumental," for a moment forgetting they have kids. He rebuilds Devil's Tower in his living room. In the end, Roy flies away aboard the Mother Ship, never to be seen again. I've become obsessed with the movie over the years.

Mom and Cheryl went to *Kramer vs. Kramer.* Dustin Hoffman plays the husband of a cold, aloof woman, and the father of an annoying boy. The wife, played by Meryl Streep in her chilliest performance, leaves her family, allows them to bond without her, and returns to make them unhappy all over again.

"I hate movies. They always portray the woman as the villain," Mom said.

Divorcing wasn't her idea. Dad played the Meryl Steep character in our situation, swooping in on weekends to take us kids away. *Kramer vs. Kramer* told a thinly veiled version of Mom's recent life story in 105 minutes.

I went with Dad to see *All That Jazz* about a cheating, womanizing Broadway musical director who sleeps with one chorus girl after another and dies youngish, leaving a handsome corpse. Dad loved it. I did too. I had a serious crush on the Broadway director's young dancer daughter.

A year later, I went with Mom to see *Ordinary People*, an eventual Best Picture Oscar winner directed by Robert Redford. Timothy Hutton plays a suicidal teenager struggling to cope with the drowning of his older brother. The mom, played brilliantly and once again in chilly fashion (this time by Mary Tyler Moore), has lost her capacity to love her surviving son. Her husband, played by Donald Sutherland, confronts her. She moves out, leaving father and son to seek comfort alone.

Mom had read the novel. What was she thinking? Another week of grumpiness followed. I wish I could have rented *The Grapes of Wrath*, but those were pre-home-video days. Too bad *Forrest Gump* didn't exist yet. It's the ultimate Mother's Day and worst Father's Day movie ever.

MY RELATIONSHIP with Dad, after he left, began to wither. He dated a fellow real estate agent (real estate something-or-other being his newfound occupation). I don't know the woman's name. I don't know if he ever told me her name and I didn't care if he had. So, I'll refer to her as Vera (inspired by the movie *Detour* because, well, why not? It's a great movie and she's a magnificent character described by Roger Ebert as a "venomous castrator").

Vera and I met one time, at his apartment for dinner—Cheryl and me and him and her. She was a curvaceous woman. *What does he see in her? She's disgusting*, I wondered, maybe out loud.

"My, you're a quiet one," she said.

My, you're a fatty, I thought.

"You should spend time with your dad. He misses you."

You should mind your own damn business.

And on it went.

I'm ashamed of how I treated her. I wish I'd at least visited enough times to learn her name. The one-sided banter between her and me is suggestive. Bruised by divorce, I struck out at whomever Dad dared place before me. Her words, though, conveyed nothing but concern and love for him. The reality of what he'd done soon set in. He held back tears. He needed her to help them flow, in private.

Years later, I visited him and his second wife (a different woman). He remained composed. His wife told me a week later he'd sobbed in her arms for half an hour after my departing car turned the corner.

~panic took hold~

I WISHED it to be a portal to another planet, but my bean bag chair wasn't magical. I needed to find a practical way to escape. Throughout my youth, one of my favorite pastimes was wading through California ocean shore tide pools at El Capitan State Beach and Campground, a fourteen-mile jaunt from Goleta. Cheryl and I would head straight to the barnacle-covered rocks and spend all morning brushing away seaweed to see what we might find. People are squeamish about tide pools. Sea anemones, crabs, and starfish can be squishy, pinchy, and squirty. But I'd examine anything. I'd visit aquariums and hold sea cucumbers. They're the softest, floppiest things you ever felt. I dreamed of handling one in the wild.

As my final year of high school slogged along, I started to map out my future by planning to become a marine biologist. I'd spend my days swimming in the ocean, the largest tide pool of them all. The leading school of marine biology in the state, the University of California at San Diego, accepted me. It wasn't its academic prospects I found appealing. It was the distance. You had to drive all the way through scary Los Angeles and beyond. I could forget all about Sue and no longer worry about Mom pushing me into embarrassing phone calls with Kimberly.

I enrolled in a scuba diving class. I needed to learn how to spend hours deep underwater without dying. The lessons started out in my favor. We had a book with tables to memorize and formulas to grasp. Classmates squirmed in their seats. I happily sat and crunched numbers.

The training moved to an indoor swimming pool. I was still enjoying myself, until it happened—the moment where all my classmates kept swimming while I started to sink. In scuba diving class, one skill must be mastered: clearing a mask. Your head can bump against a rock and jar your mask loose, causing it to flood. When that happens, you remove the water by pressing the top of the mask against your forehead and blowing air out through your nostrils.

Sounds easy, but I couldn't do it. I'd blow out through my mouth. I'd inhale through my nose. I'd feel as if I were about to drown. I'd panic.

"You'll get it," the instructor's lips said while his expression said, *Oh shit.*

Most students in my class were couples—young couples my age, adult couples, and a pair of grandparents. Clearing masks became child's play for all of them. The guy would flood and clear his mask while she watched. She'd do the same. They'd high-five.

The class hit the beach in full scuba regalia: wet suit, weight belt, and big, floppy fins. Trudging across the deep, loose sand to the awaiting surf exhausted me. I walked backward into the waves, the foamy water shoved me back toward the shore (the ocean trying to tell me something), and I waded until I could swim. Beneath the kelp beds, the ocean floor drops off from a depth of five to fifteen feet.

"I need you all to descend until you're sitting on the bottom. Flood your mask and clear it. I'll watch you, one at a time," the instructor said.

When my turn arrived, I took a deep breath from my regulator and pulled my mask away from my face. The cold, cloudy water made me claustrophobic. I tried to follow the procedure, but panic took hold. I nearly passed out. The instructor swam me to the surface. Along the way, he punched me in the chest to force air out of my lungs.

I spent the remainder of the lesson treading water and watching couples play in the surf. For the graduation trip to Santa Cruz Island (already paid for), I swallowed Dramamine and tagged along. I didn't lug a heavy air tank. I spent the day snorkeling on the surface while the graduates cruised along the bottom, twenty feet below me.

Mom and Dad seemed relieved by my misfortune. I

canceled my plans to move to San Diego and become a marine biologist. I wouldn't be moving far away after all. This made Mom happy, which surprised me. I thought she considered me a pathetic disappointment. How could she be happy I'd found yet another way to fail? Dad had paid for the scuba lessons. He was off the hook for paying for San Diego as well.

"I knew you didn't have it in you," he said.

I do still wish I'd stuck with marine biology. There are many ways to study life in the ocean besides scouring its floor. I could've sat in a lab and peered into a microscope. And Dad was right about my not having it in me. I recently took a course in swimming pool lifesaving. I had to float on my back while the instructor demonstrated how to immobilize my neck to prevent additional injury as he swam me to the edge of the pool. Each time water washed over my face, he noted I tensed up.

"You're not comfortable in the water, are you?" he said.

Failing scuba diving class changed the course of my life. It may have saved it. If I'd managed to fake my way through mask clearing and joined the graduates in their frolicking with the fish, I may have one day snagged my mask on the Great Barrier Reef, panicked, drowned, and gotten gobbled by sharks, all set to the music John Williams composed for *Jaws*.

Nope. Fate had something else in store for me.

~movie-making magic~

AND BACK to my high school reality I went. I abandoned future career Plan A. I ditched it quickly and easily. Soon Plan B took its equally temporary shape in my mind.

One day in the band room, sitting in my third section trumpet chair oiling my valves, preparing to fake it through fifty minutes of band practice while watching Sue out of the corner of my eye, I overheard two fellow trumpeters talking.

"What do you think?" one said.

"About what?" his buddy said before blowing spit from his valves into a puddle on the floor.

"The Oscars. Who do you think is gonna win? De Niro or Voight?"

"De Niro. He was great."

"*The Deer Hunter* was amazing, but I think it'll go to Voight. They love to give Oscars to people playing cripples and shit."

"Yeah, you're probably right."

The band director, Ike Jenkins, flew into the room in a flurry of excitement, animated as usual, but over-the-top. He told us a friend was friends with a friend of John Heard and he and his friend had spoken over a few beers. We'd been invited to be extras in a movie.

"Who is John Heard?" someone asked.

"Who else is in it?" someone else chimed.

"Jeff Bridges," Ike said.

"Ooh," our majorette, Yvonne, said with a sigh.

"All I know is it's called *Cutter and Bone* and they need a marching band for a parade scene," Ike continued.

You could hear a pin before it dropped. *Cutter? Bone? What horror flick are we getting ourselves into?*

Our scene re-created an Old Spanish Days Fiesta parade.

We gathered after school on our football practice field and recorded a marching tune, the name of which I've long forgotten. A soundman organized us into small groups around a bunch of microphones. It freaked me out. The sole trumpeter at my station, I couldn't hide. Luckily, everyone else around my microphone also sat third section something-or-other. Ike probably did that on purpose and whispered to the sound guy to leave the microphone off.

Yvonne played percussion when not twirling a baton and she insisted on tapping a cymbal during the recording session. She wanted to be a major part of our Jeff Bridges experience. On the soundtrack, there's a distinctive rhythmic ringing emanating, not from any musician in the parade, but from the sparkly girl leading the charge. Such is movie-making magic.

The recording session went on for hours. We never wanted to hear the song ever again, let alone play it. And happily, we didn't play it again. When filmed in the parade in full uniform, our faces dabbed with makeup, only the drummers played, tapping lightly on their rims to keep us in step. The rest of us pretended. It felt ridiculous.

I remember lots of starting and stopping and standing around while people near the camera argued and adjusted dolly tracks, smoke machines, and light reflectors. At one point, we marched fast, then slow. The pseudo-parade consisted of us, a few cars with politicians, and two floats. The director singled Yvonne out for something special. He prominently displayed her well ahead of us.

Caught up in the excitement of making a movie, my head filled with ideas.

WHENEVER I needed to escape, I'd visit Aunt Gwen in Oxnard. After my brush with Jeff Bridges, I had something to tell her. I planned to move to Hollywood and find work.

I hopped into my VW and hit the freeway. I made the forty-minute drive to her house on the outskirts of town, with nothing around it except strawberry fields for miles. Most of the drive was pleasant and traffic-free, but as Oxnard came into view, the number of cars became nerve-racking. Beyond Aunt Gwen's house and those strawberries, a huge uphill grade ascended. Beyond, in my mind, one thing lurked: scary, zombie-filled Los Angeles.

As I pulled into her driveway, Aunt Gwen stepped outside to greet me.

"Aunt Gwen! Aunt Gwen! I want to make movies! I've decided to move to Hollywood after I graduate."

She looked at me for a moment as if I'd announced plans to join the circus. (I see images of Steve Martin in the movie *The Jerk*, fleeing from a crazed sniper and ducking into a carnival trailer as it's about to hit the road. If I'd moved to Hollywood, which you've probably guessed I did not, I doubt I would've made it far in the movie industry. More likely, I would've been living in a trailer, munching corn dogs, and learning about my "special purpose" in all the wrong places.)

"Let's go," she said, motioning for me to hop into her beat-up yellow Plymouth Duster. Where were we going and why so quickly? I hadn't had a chance to go inside and pee yet.

A country tune by Anne Murray, "He Thinks I Still Care," warbled from a crookedly retrofitted 8-track tape deck. She listened to Murray a lot. She was a sad-country-music-song lover.

I opened the glove box and sifted through it, a rolling junk drawer. Bottles of aspirin and Tums slid about. I glimpsed a brush filled with her hair strands. A used-up can of Right Guard missing its cap fell out. I caught it and tossed it back in. It made my hands gunky, and I wiped them on my shorts. Two heavily read paperbacks, a Zane Grey to go along with the usual Barbara Cartland, had been smashed together with their pages interwoven. And a crushed carton of Marlboro Lights, with two packs remaining, hid in the back.

"I'm just going to dipsy-doodle a bit," she said as she bypassed the freeway.

Dipsy-doodle. It was her favorite driving expression and it still makes me laugh. She always tried to find a better way. She would search for side roads, alternative avenues, fewer stop lights, and with a jerk of the steering wheel she'd exclaim, "Ah. Dipsy-doodle time!"

As the Esplanade Mall came into view, I relaxed. Our destination was the same as always: a bookstore. Mom and Aunt Gwen devoured books. If I close my eyes and think about them at any point in my life, I always picture books nearby. Mom joined countless book groups. Scout and Atticus Finch from *To Kill a Mockingbird* (a great book about empathy) were her favorite characters. (Cheryl remembers Mom's favorite book as *The Secret Garden*. It's beautiful as well.) Aunt Gwen always sat beside a leaning tower of paperbacks.

Luckily, I inherited the book gene from them. Dad isn't a reader. I've seen him hold one book, *Papillon*, about "a man imprisoned on Devil's Island who escapes by flinging himself from a giant rock into the foaming sea to float for days in the shriveling sun." (I stole those words from the dust jacket.) I'd catch him staring at the book's cover depicting a butterfly lifting off from a broken link in a chain.

I'd observe Aunt Gwen reading. She'd rip through westerns and romance novels, flip the stack, and read them all over again. I've never seen anyone else read so many books, so fast. The sight of her kicked back in a deck chair holding a paperback with a cigarette between her knuckles fascinated me. The smoke swirling around her and weaving in and out of the pages as they fanned through her fingers seeped into my imagination. It's why I'm fascinated to this day by images of Parisian coffeehouse denizens seated at sidewalk tables with an espresso, a book, and a smoke. It's why I love movies by Jean-Luc Godard. I imagine myself reading Sartre as my mind drifts into a swirl of cream, a galaxy in the universe of my coffee cup, contemplating being and nothingness as if I'm a character from *2 or 3 Things I Know About Her*.

Aunt Gwen often spoke of books: *The Call of the Wild* and *The Adventures of Tom Sawyer*, and on one occasion, with a gleam in her eye, *The Illiad* and *The Odyssey*. The way those last two titles rolled off her tongue thrilled me. I had no idea what their pages contained. Another title I loved to hear her say: *The Rubáiyát of*

Omar Khayyám. She located an aged, red-leather-bound copy with brittle pages at Bart's in Ojai—a quaint indoor/outdoor used bookstore I still visit. (It thrilled me to see it featured in the Emma Stone movie *Easy A*.)

When we'd hit a bookstore, she'd set me free to explore and return with whatever I discovered. She'd pay for it and reward me for my fine choice by splitting a plain bagel with plain cream cheese in the café next door. She always made me feel my treasured book was wonderful and would ask if she could read it after I finished. I'd nod my head while chewing and she'd follow through. She'd read the book too, and we'd talk about it.

"I loved the part where Tom sticks his head out the train window and a cinder lodges in his eye," she said. (Tom is the hero of the *Great Brain* series about a Mormon boy who outwits the adults in his life.)

"I don't know. It made my eyes water and I stopped reading for a bit," I said.

"That's what's so great about books. They make you feel what the character is feeling. They help us understand what people are going through."

My book choices strayed far afield from her usual reading tastes. I went through a phase of mysteries, devouring the *Alfred Hitchcock and the Three Investigators* series. For a streak, I read those *Great Brain* books by John D. Fitzgerald and wanted to be Tom.

Yet far and away Edgar Rice Burroughs's fantastical adventures to nearby planets, to the center of the Earth, and into the depths of the African jungle most captivated me. Those stories offered my boyishly introverted mind the heroic and exotic escape it craved. One year for my birthday, Aunt Gwen spent days and countless attempts at perfecting an acrylic painting, a reproduction of Frank Frazetta's *Land of Terror* cover depicting David Innes of Pellucidar running an alligator through the heart with a spear. (I'm staring at it on my wall as I type.)

I'm surprised she chose an Edgar Rice Burroughs book cover as the subject of a painting. She knew I loved them, and it was a birthday gift, but every time she'd catch me standing in the bookstore staring at one of the covers with either Jane or Dejah featured prominently, she'd furrow her brow.

"Why do artists always paint them with so little clothing you can see their *boo-boos*?" she'd say, mostly to herself.

I pondered why Aunt Gwen had chosen to talk about *The Great Brain at the Academy*. We hadn't read it for several years. Her mind seemed far away. I tried to change the subject to something current.

"I read *Jungle Tales of Tarzan* again last week. The story where there's an eclipse and all the savages think Tarzan is a god is so cool. It's how myths begin."

She ignored my diversion.

"Todd. How're things going?"

"Oh, fine. A month to go and I'll finally be out of high school."

"You know what I mean. Your mom is worried about you and girls. Is that why you want to do something silly like go to Hollywood?"

(At that moment, I knew she and Mom had been on the phone while I'd spent forty minutes on the freeway.)

"Do we have to talk about it?"

"I hear you got all tongue-tied on the phone with…what's her name?"

"Kimberly."

"What are you afraid of? Just talk to girls the way you talk to me. You're a terrific guy."

"I never know what to say. Girls hate Tarzan and Pellucidar."

"How do you know? You have to talk to them to get to know them. Think of talking to girls as like reading books. You didn't know anything at all about Tom before you read about him. Now your eyes water when his eyes water. Isn't that cool?"

"I guess so."

"But you came all this way to talk about Hollywood and movies. Why?"

"I got to be in one. I spent two days marching around in a circle pretending to play my trumpet. There was this huge camera on the street corner as we went by."

"Sounds exciting." Her sarcasm was obvious, intentionally so. We both laughed.

"Okay. It was boring. There was a picture of me yawning on the front page of the newspaper." (My fellow bandmates teased me about it for days.)

"It does sound boring. So, why do you want to move to Hollywood? Do you think everything's going to be different once you get there? You'll still be the same old Todd."

"I need to do something."

"Have you seen *The Wizard of Oz*?"

"Of course."

"What does Dorothy try to do?"

"She runs away from home trying to find a better place."

"Does she?"

"No. She learns there's no place like home."

I DROVE back to Goleta and, as the traffic lessened past Oxnard, calmness settled over me. I'd once again fled from my troubles, but, same as the frigid ocean waters had conspired to keep me away from San Diego, traffic and Aunt Gwen's *Wizard of Oz* analogy denied me Los Angeles as well. I'd twice tried to head in the wrong direction and something out there—or inside me—turned me around. Back home, I kicked back on my bed and Hollywood dreams faded. My future emptied. Instead of hooking up with Ben Kenobi and heading out to a Mos Eisley Cantina, Luke Skywalker was turning his back on those two suns and returning to his workshop to continue repairing farming droids.

Those two fellow trumpeters I overheard talking about the Oscars both moved to Hollywood after graduating from high school. One became a writer and producer of the television shows *Nash Bridges*, *The Pretender*, and *CSI: Crime Scene Investigation.* The other vanished.

Years later, I watched *Cutter's Way*. Our scene has John Heard standing on the curb watching the parade. He wears a funny black hat and eye patch. A cigarette dangles from his mouth. As Yvonne struts past him, wearing a tight-fitting, sparkly gold and blue majorette outfit with her baton dancing about her neck and shoulders, he wonders out loud to Jeff Bridges what such girlies do with those smooth, polished chrome batons.

I wanted to punch him in the face. I hoped Yvonne would never see the movie and, if she did, she'd take solace that the crude words emanated from John Heard and not Jeff Bridges.

~a silly place~

MY ESCAPE plans had gone from San Diego to Hollywood to sticking around and going nowhere. Or I *did* go somewhere: The University of California at Santa Barbara. It had its appeal. I could step out of class and onto the beach. And while it wasn't Hollywood, I would soon discover it had a fledgling Film Studies department. I moved my record collection and a few belongings two miles to a huge, off-campus dorm—two towering buildings crowded with a thousand rowdy freshmen who did nothing but party.

Plan C: Mechanical Engineer. I'd never given the career any thought. I had no idea what engineers did, but I'd enroll in lots of math and science classes along the way, two of my favorite subjects. I imagine I would've been happier watching plankton through a lab microscope or cutting cheap horror films for Troma, but my new course was set.

My quiet South Korean roommate, Mike Kim, shielded me from the partying. (He kept assuring me I couldn't pronounce his Korean name. He had trouble with my name as well. He always called me "Dodd.") I also had my headphones. Pink Floyd, Bruce Springsteen, and the Stones entered my collection. I spent my freshman year in endless cycles of "sleeping," nodding off during classes, and spinning records to drown out the neighbors' noise.

Near the end of the fall semester, I returned to our dorm room late one night after a library cram session. I turned on my bedside lamp and thumbed through my LPs, needing something to take the edge off.

"What will it be," I asked out loud, "*Some Girls*? *Darkness on the Edge of Town*? *Animals*?"

I chose *Darkness*, pulled it out of the sleeve, dropped it onto the turntable, and reached for my headphones. I heard a pencil drop upon a desktop. *Plunk.*

I walked over to Mike's side of the two-sided desk which served as a room divider. He sat in the dark staring at a writing pad, the page blank except for a few crossed out scribbles. He twirled the pencil.

"Fortran. I can't understand Fortran," he said, avoiding my eyes.

"Don't worry. You'll get it," I said.

"No, you don't get it, Dodd. I don't get it. I don't know what I'll d-do if I can't get it."

I stood quietly for a moment. We were immersed in a required course in the fundamentals of programming. Computers fascinated me. Coding is all about looping and branching—doing the same thing repeatedly and occasionally using IF/ELSE statements to explore different paths. (Two years later, Mike helped me survive an electrical engineering class—his turn to shake me as I slumped at *my* desk.)

He'd struggled and managed to pass the quizzes and tests and write the tiny sample programs, but this exceeded his ability to muddle through. On his night of despair, we had been assigned our big final project: The Knight's Tour. You had to set up a chessboard in memory, have a knight start out on a random square, and have the playing piece make random knight moves until it could no longer do so without landing on an already visited square. The program had to print out a record of what the knight had done. Those were the days before desktop computers. Programming didn't mean banging your fingers—and head—against a keyboard, compiling, and praying. It meant writing out your program on paper, riding your bike to the computer lab, sitting at a punch station keying a stack of instruction cards, running them through a reader, and banging your head against a wall while praying.

"Let's write the program together," I suggested.

"Dodd, I have to be able to do this. What if I have to d-do this on the job someday?"

"Well, give me a call and we'll do it together, again."

"Well—"

"No 'well.' Turn your light on," I said, rolling my chair over to his desk.

We spent the next few days writing, bike riding, keying, straightening out card stacks, and feeding them into the reader. We'd stand back and pray. Our knights would fail to step on stage. They'd exit the board and head to Camelot (which is a silly place). They'd jump around aimlessly, re-landing on the same square until the mainframe angrily threw an error. (While at IBM, Dad had installed the computer. It knew how to be grumpy.)

After many false starts, Mike fed his cards through the reader and stepped back. It ran for a while. The wide, white-and-green striped sheets of paper clicked out of the printer. No red error messages marred the output. An eight-by-eight grid showed the successful tour his knight had completed. He couldn't believe it.

"My turn," I said, clutching my nearly identical stack of cards.

As I walked toward the reader, I tripped, and the cards flew from my hand. Around two hundred slippery suckers slid everywhere, many irretrievably beneath the mainframe. We surveyed the catastrophe. We laughed till Mike cried.

For our second year of college, Mike and I moved into a less crowded two-story dorm pleasantly named Tropicana Gardens. There was far less partying (that we could hear). We had a socially inept roommate, a third wheel named Allen, who kept to himself and half-assedly studied economics. We made a perfect trio. Mike moved a desk into our closet so he could study 24/7 without keeping me awake at night. He soon moved his bed in as well. It gave amusing meaning to "walk-in" closet. (And if you're trying to imagine the geometry, don't worry. It was indeed a huge walk-in closet and the beds were twin-size.) Allen and I spent our evenings holed up in our living room listening to King Crimson, Genesis, and Yes and playing never-ending games of *Risk* using a world map covering our entire living room floor. Chance of girls ever wandering into *our* world: zero.

For year three, Mike and I shared an apartment. His desk

and bed occupied the bedroom. My matching set relocated to the living room with the couch pushed into a corner. A giant Italian poster for *A Clockwork Orange* watched me as I slept. Mike still studied all day and all night. South Korean male culture and the taboo of academic failure must be stifling.

Those years of me going nowhere fast remind me of one of the few concepts I learned in college:

in·er·tia

a tendency to do nothing
or to remain unchanged

~ a perfect escape ~

LET'S REWIND my movie back to freshman year in college, when the Film Studies department caught my attention. I was hanging out in my dorm's community lounge on a Sunday evening, waiting to seize control of the television to watch Carl Sagan's *Cosmos* (yeah, that's about as crazy as I got), when I overheard two students talking about a new class offering: "Intro to Film Studies."

"It's an easy A," one said.

(I managed a B+.)

"All you have to do is watch movies," his friend said.

I'd seen a few dozen movies, a go-catch-*Superman*-while-munching-popcorn kind of guy, but I'd never watched a foreign language film. Soon, *The Searchers*, *Rashomon*, and *Citizen Kane* entranced me—aided by the infectious enthusiasm of Professor Chuck Wolfe.

My life shifted. I filled my electives and free moments with film studies courses and art films. I saw a lot of Federico Fellini. I delved into Ingmar Bergman as well. Why didn't I change my major?

in·er·tia

a property of matter by which it continues in its existing state of rest or uniform motion

MOVIES HAVE always waited in my wings. They're a perfect escape for introverted boys (and a perfect thing to lure a reluctant engineering student away from his studies). My friend

Tommy (the owner of Princess's namesake cat) couldn't wait for his ninth birthday to arrive. He celebrated on a Sunday afternoon, with me and his other best friend, Johnny, at the movies. No adults allowed. We'd officially grown up. We saw *Willy Wonka and the Chocolate Factory* at the sprawling Arlington Theater. It felt cavernous to a nine-year-old.

I've already lovingly described the theater while writing about seeing *Star Wars*, but I wasn't aware of any of those star-twinkling details during my earlier Wonka visit. I cowered. I'd never been to a movie with *or* without Mom and Dad. Living in a home that forbade *Batman*, a darkened theater felt spookier than a real Batcave. My two pals dashed about making popcorn runs. I sat with legs pulled to my chest.

The recruiting of the Golden Ticket-winning kids kept me in my comfort zone—except for the freaky guy with a scar who kept whispering into the kids' ears. The song "Cheer up, Charlie" relaxed me and I placed my feet back on the floor, but my comfort didn't last. Mr. Wonka looked CREEPY and by the time the Wonka-boat entered the Wonka-tunnel and slithering creatures started coming at me from all Wonka-directions, my knees hit my chin and my hands covered my eyes. I believe I hid my disgraceful behavior from my friends thanks to the darkness and on-screen distractions, but they never again invited me to a movie.

The shift in tone from anger to overflowing happiness during the final scene when poor Charlie places the Everlasting Gobstopper on Wonka's desk affected me. It made all the prior terrors worthwhile. Memories of those feelings still bring tears to my eyes.

If I'd been a child during home video days, movies might have filled my daydreams instead of books. I might've been fantasizing about Jane Fonda instead of Jane Porter. Janie might've twirled in my door frame and said, "You sure have lots of movies. Which are your favorites?"

"Oh, *Willy Wonka and the Chocolate Factory*—no, *The Wizard of Oz*," I might have said.

In 1982, I watched Spielberg's *E.T.: The Extra-Terrestrial* countless times. After waiting in line for a sneak preview, I returned once a week until its run ended. It enchanted me: a boy—shy, introverted, and struggling to cope with divorce, living with busy mom while trying to keep in touch with wayward dad. I was watching myself. The sequence I awaited each time is the one where Elliot goes to school and E.T. remains at home. With perfectly timed slapstick, E.T. drinks Coors, dribbling all over himself, and Elliot kisses the prettiest girl in his class.

During my early cinema-obsessed days, I would watch Brian De Palma's *Dressed to Kill* endlessly. The way the camera glides about an art museum as Angie Dickinson and a dark-haired stranger engage in a cat-and-mouse game of seduction wasn't what so captivated me. The scene where Nancy Allen wears black lingerie didn't keep me coming back. (Okay, it did.) What most fascinated me was the short sequence where Keith Gordon uses a stopwatch, does some math, and employs a camera to make a time-lapse movie of clients arriving at and departing from Michael Caine's psychiatrist's office. The same feelings flowed through me a year later while watching John Travolta animate a car crashing into a pond in De Palma's *Blow Out* by cutting up a magazine and clicking pictures of the still images, his creation coming to life when he adds his sound recording. Those scenes are ecstatic nuts-and-bolts cinema. They showed me two geeky guys using their smarts and a camera to gain a bit of control over their puzzling lives.

During my final year of college, I worked in a snack shop at a golf course with two girls, both named Sue. (Well, one went by Suzie. Why did they have to be named Sue?) Suzie would flirt with me. I decided to follow Aunt Gwen's advice and share a bit of myself with her. Under the spell of having seen a string of artsy movies—Bergman, Fellini, Buñuel—I imagined, as I stocked the beer cooler and scraped the grill, a scene I wanted to write and direct. It involved a formal dinner with faceless but cultured guests and servants and four elaborate courses—all taking place on a windy, rainy, rocky seashore and no matter how mightily any of the guests tried to do so, they couldn't escape.

"Can I ask you something?" I said to Suzie.

"Yes," she said, pausing from restocking the Doritos.

I described to her the scene in my head.

"Well, what do you think?" I asked.

She never again flirted with me. It was going to take a miracle for me to ever manage fathering children. I certainly wouldn't score using pickup lines inspired by *The Discreet Charm of the Bourgeoisie*.

Unperturbed (either that or Suzie never told Sue about our moment), Sue asked me if I'd drive her home, saying her car had a flat and her sister had driven her to work.

"Okay," I said.

"I'll grab my purse."

We hopped into my VW. No girl except Cheryl had ever occupied my passenger seat before. During the half-mile drive, she fiddled with my radio, which annoyed me. It had been tuned to my favorite station.

When I arrived in front of her house, I noticed her car parked in the driveway. All the tires looked fine.

"Someone must've fixed your tire," I said.

"Yeah, I guess so," she said, looking at me, waiting.

"See you later," I said.

"Bye," she said.

She walked into her house. I drove home. No girl besides Cheryl sat in my VW's passenger seat ever again.

I was an idiot.

~learning about chemistry~

I'M ROLLING my footage back one more time (this is fun) to me at age nineteen, when I first asked a woman for her phone number. I took the freshman year required math course for mechanical engineering: Calculus I. I didn't struggle with the concepts, but the number of homework problems daunted me. A few of us would gather in the community lounge at my dorm to divvy them up. We also soon realized the practical value of sharing phone numbers. We wrote them on the inside covers of our calculus textbooks. I'd see the names every time I opened the cover: Marc, Jim, and…LeeAnne.

Marc and I had been buds as kids, first grade and second grade. To this day, the one time I've ever held or fired a gun was his BB gun in his backyard shooting at Coke cans. We'd play one-on-one football every day after school on his front yard lawn, toy NFL helmets and all. He'd be the Cowboys. I'd be the Rams.

Around third grade, I screwed it all up. For his birthday, I gave him a copy of one of my favorite books, *Fantastic Mr. Fox*. Others gave him bags of candy. Not long after, our class at school held a contest to see who could most creatively decorate a bowling pin. He'd transformed his into a dapper mouse with clothing cut from bits of felt, fastidiously glued into place. On the due date, he had a dental appointment (I believe), so he left the mouse with me to bring to class. During the night, all the glue released its hold. When I awoke and sat in bed, I saw a naked bowling pin with bits of felt cluttering the top of my dresser. I tried to glue the clothes back in place but failed miserably. His gentleman looked tousled. Upon arriving at school (he'd been forewarned), he could barely contain his rage as he scooped the mess and retreated to a corner table to repair my damage. My own bowling pin resembled nothing recognizable. It was modern art. He accused me of being jealous and wrecking his masterpiece intentionally. Friendship canceled.

During high school, we moved in different circles, or he moved in a circle—played soccer, chased girls, drank, and passed out on the lawns of complete strangers—and I occupied a point—sat in my car during lunch doing math homework, daydreamed in my bean bag chair, and read Tarzan novels. To him, I no longer existed. I'd catch glimpses of him at school, from time to time, and sigh.

A surprise to both of us, we locked eyes across the room at a freshman college gathering. He held a can of Coors, assuredly. I fumbled my matching beverage, dribbling down my chest like E.T. every time I took a sip. We both laughed—at me.

Jim, a loadie-turned-"serious"-student, partook in *shrooms* and seeing how long he could *last* in a hot tub with his girlfriend before he *busted a nut.* (It was all a foreign language to me.) Honestly, I don't remember Jim in detail. LeeAnne, though, is a different story. I will never un-remember her.

She was a delightful Japanese American woman, always a pleasure to eat pizza with while struggling over math problems and pounding beers. I didn't know she existed, until one day, from out of nowhere, she sat a few seats away in a crowded lecture hall learning about chemistry. I looked her way for a beat too long. She turned, smiled, and said, "Hi. I'm LeeAnne. This class is blowing my mind."

"Yeah," I said. "This stuff was so much easier in high school."

She laughed. I laughed. And we became study partners for life. Well, for college life anyway.

WE FOUR amigos took a trip across the border into Mexico to smuggle cheap booze back into the States—my criminal phase, which lasted two days.

Okay. I did have two other lawless episodes. One came during a Strength of Materials group project. We were tasked with building a structure out of computer punch cards. The competing structures would be placed in a compression test machine. The winning team would be the designers of the structure able to withstand the most compression before crushing per ounce the structure weighed.

I popped open a third beer, volunteered to gather the needed supplies, and hopped on my bicycle. I snuck into the computer lab, found it empty, and stole away with an entire unopened box of punch cards. With the box under my left arm and steering with my right hand while still holding my beer, somehow, I began my slow trek back to Marc's apartment. I'd managed about five rotations of my pedals when I found my path blocked by three campus bicycle cops. They wanted to hear my story and assured me it better be good. I've never been an articulate drunk. I'm positive they found my story unconvincing, but it made them laugh; they asked me to hand over the loot and sent me on my wobbly way. Ironically, the winning structure used a single punch card rolled into a tube.

I perpetrated my other crime during my senior year at UCSB while working at that infamous golf course snack shop. I finished cleaning the grill at the end of a trying day and thought, *Now's the perfect time to find out what this smoking thing is all about.* I palmed a pack of Marlboros and a box of matches and headed out back by the dumpster. I tore the pack open, gave the cigs a whiff, considered aborting, but decided to carry on. I thought about sticking two in my mouth at once because it always looks cool when heroes do it in movies, but instead plucked one out of the pack and placed it between my lips. I struck a match, lit up, took a drag, coughed, exhaled, felt the smoke fill my nostrils, and winced. I hadn't expected pain to accompany the pleasure. I tossed the cigarette on the ground and stomped on it, flipped the rest of the pack into the dumpster, and drove home sneezing with eyes watering.

(I'll never understand why Aunt Gwen smoked two, three packs a day.)

Anyway, back at the U.S./Mexico border, Law permitted us to return to the States with two bottles each. The four of us stashed five cases under a blanket in the trunk. My criminal cohorts had it all worked out. We had a bag of oranges on the back seat, and they insisted I drive when we went through the border inspection because I looked innocent.

When I came to a stop, the officer asked, "Are you kids bringing anything back from your stay?"

"No," I said. "Oh, wait." I reached into the back seat and grabbed the bag of oranges and showed them to him.

"I'll have to take those," he said.

"Can I keep just one?"

"Sorry, son," he said as I handed the bag over. He waved us through.

We imagined ourselves as gangsters. I imagine the officer thinking, *Hmm, four college kids. A full case of booze apiece in the trunk, but I don't care. I get kickbacks from every liquor store in Tijuana.*

Marc and LeeAnne sat in the front seats, talking.

"Come on LeeAnne, please," Marc said. "The team is short one player."

"But I've never played soccer before."

"It's easy and fun. I played varsity in high school. I can show you everything I know."

"I'd like that."

"So would I."

Jim and I sat in the back. He smelled the way the Arlington Theater had when I watched *Pink Floyd: Live at Pompeii.* I stared out the window and thought about the boy, not more than five or six, we'd seen in Tijuana in an empty early morning street trying to sell us tattered *Playboy* magazines.

(My early morning Tijuana street memory reminds me of another *Playboy* magazine moment. For my eighteenth birthday, Mom surprised me—and I mean startled me—with a gift subscription to the magazine. She hated *Playboy* and everything it stood for and implied. She gave the word "porn" an interesting twist by mispronouncing it as "forn." She'd study my reaction as I removed each monthly issue from its brown paper wrapper, hoping I formed ideas that might one day lead to her having grandchildren.)

One evening, my drinking buddies and I played quarters with Killian's Red. LeeAnne sat on the couch alone, finding our game not to her liking. Each time I plucked the quarter and prepared to bounce it into a glass, I glanced over at her and wondered if I should duck out of the game and go sit beside her. On my third glance, she was gone.

We guys took a break and sped off on our bicycles to catch an on-campus screening of *Night of the Living Dead* (yeah, my idea). I made an unintended side trip down a flight of concrete stairs on my bicycle in the darkness. Unbelievably, I didn't fall or crash. I laughed hysterically. As we pedaled toward the lecture hall, we learned the screening had sold out. We turned around and headed back to Marc's apartment. After we arrived, sat at the kitchen table, and the smell of beer and potato chips hit my nostrils, I felt suddenly nauseated. I left without saying a word, walked outside, and "fed the shrubs" with (it looked and felt like) everything I'd eaten during the past four years. By the time I'd crawled to my apartment, I'd spewed out everything I'd eaten in my life. Lying on the bathroom floor all night, I realized I hadn't needed to see a movie about zombies because I had become one, except I wasn't among the walking dead. I curled around the toilet bowl wishing I *was* dead. I wished I had ducked out of playing quarters and spent the evening with LeeAnne.

Something else happened. Mike never opened his bedroom door. As I lay on the cool tiles, he didn't visit our bathroom, not once. Didn't he need to pee? In the morning, as I sat on the couch cradling my head, he emerged, for a moment.

"D-d-dodd. You shouldn't get d-d-d-drunk. It's not a D-doddly thing to d-do and you'll regret it."

He'd never been nervous around me before and I'd barely detected his stutter. He retreated, closing the door again, leaving an air of betrayal behind. And he still hadn't peed. We remained close for the remainder of our college days and for a while beyond, but our roommate situation ended along with our junior year.

For my twenty-first birthday, my few engineering buddies threw me a keg party complete with swimming pool, tequila (yes,

I swallowed the worm), and Bob Marley (my latest discovery).

I didn't know Marc and LeeAnne had been dating. I didn't know lots of things. I'd invited her to the party. She'd declined saying she felt too sore from playing soccer and would see me later. Her not being there meant I relaxed. I swam, drank tequila, and danced to reggae—all at the same time.

I awoke late the next morning feeling run over by the truck that'd hauled the worm, tequila-and-all, over the border. I considered breakfast. My friends insisted Taco Bell would cure my ailment. My stomach did a flip-flop and I instead drove to Mom's condo with a load of laundry. I walked in and headed straight for the washer with my basket. As I dumped my underwear, socks, T-shirts, and jeans into the machine, I glanced to the left through the kitchen and saw Mom seated at the dining room table, staring into a coffee mug. I noticed something else. Princess hadn't greeted me at the door.

"Mom. Where—?"

"Todd," she said, still looking at her coffee, her voice trembling. "I wish you'd come home yesterday. I tried to—"

I no longer heard her words. I slid to the floor. A sweatshirt landed in my lap. I clutched it and buried my face in its folds. Somehow, I didn't puke.

I had been consumed by my party and missed Princess's final hours. She'd had a seizure. Mom had waited for me to stop by her condo, a few hundred feet from where my party took place. (Those were days long before cell phones.) She had taken Princess to the vet without me. My dog had cancer, and was put to sleep on the spot. Mom kept quiet the rest of the day and night. She didn't want to ruin my birthday.

I'd never felt emptier in my life. I fetched my Numerical Analysis book (a math class where you use computers to solve tricky engineering problems), opened the front cover, and looked at the names and phone numbers, a tradition we'd continued throughout our college years. I sat and drew circles around LeeAnne's number for an hour like a computer program stuck in a loop.

~i watched her pedal away~

I RAN my finger across the buttons, pressed all but the last digit of LeeAnne's number, and stopped. I tried again. I panicked again. Asking LeeAnne for a date terrified me. I'd called her before, often, to compare answers on math assignments. Differential Equations had kicked both our butts.

I gave up. I figured I'd recover from my hangover and try again. Two weeks later, I was still "recovering." We met at Marc's apartment, the usual four of us, eating pizza and group-conquering math problems. I flipped through my textbook, scribbled in my notebook, glanced at LeeAnne, and took another bite of pizza. I sipped Coors, without dribbling—a senior now, long over my beer awkwardness.

"You sure are quiet today," LeeAnne said, kicking me under the table. "This must be easy for you. You enjoyed Fortran."

"No. I mean yes…um," I mumbled. There was nothing easy about homework that day. My mind idled at an IF statement. IF she indicates any interest at all, ask her out.

LeeAnne and I left together. Or, rather, she left, and I followed. Our bicycles leaned locked to a tree outside the apartment. LeeAnne and I spun our dials.

"Umm, LeeAnne," I said.

"Yes." (She may as well have said, "TRUE.")

"Would you like to see a movie?"

"You and me?"

"Yeah."

"Umm," she said, glancing back at Marc's apartment door.

"There's a Steve Martin comedy playing. I hear it's funny."

"Well," she said, glancing at the apartment again, "okay."

"How about tomorrow afternoon?"

"Sure," she said while pulling open her lock.

I watched her pedal away.

We went to *All of Me* with Steve Martin and Lily Tomlin. We drove separately. I arrived fifteen minutes early, paid, and went inside. She bought her ticket while the trailers played. The movie screened at the Fairview Theater in Goleta, the walls covered by ripped one-sheets, the carpet stained and moldy, the popcorn burnt. The place reeked of "butter."

We never touched. I kept wondering, *Should I hold her hand? Should I put my arm around her shoulders? What does one do on a date?*

I didn't laugh. Why? I've always loved Steve Martin.

LeeAnne didn't laugh either, not once. Martin and Tomlin make a classic team. It's an "out of the bottle" type movie where a bit of magic happens. Tomlin dies and takes over half of Martin's body and embarrassing comedic situations ensue. At one point, Martin orders Tomlin to assist his "Little Fireman" before he pisses all over her side of his body. Every time something R-rated happened, LeeAnne shifted in her seat, but Marc had told me on the soccer field LeeAnne could "trash talk with the best of them." When we hung out, and when Jim talked about not *busting a nut* in his hot tub, she became one of the guys, laughing and drinking along with all of it.

Our leaving the theater involved few words.

"See you in class tomorrow."

"See ya."

Later, I went out to grab a burger and rode by Marc's apartment to ask him to join me. As I approached, I noticed LeeAnne's bike once again snugly locked to the tree. I forgot the burger joint and headed home.

The trio went on a ski trip, but I bowed out.

"Family commitment," I lied.

I spent the weekend watching *Taxi Driver*, twice, at the hole-in-the-wall Magic Lantern revival theater in Isla Vista. As Robert De Niro's character, Travis Bickle, slouched in a squalid grindhouse peering at the pulsating screen through his fingers, I lost track of where his surroundings ended and mine began. We merged as one lonely man. (I still think of a bicycle locked to a tree and going home hungry every time I watch the movie.)

I laugh at my naïveté. LeeAnne and Marc had a thing going—it soon ended, and they went their separate ways—and I'd put LeeAnne on the spot. She'd had to juggle a study partner who was a boyfriend and me, a guy who wanted to be her boyfriend, whom she still wanted for a study partner. It shouldn't have been as complicated as that sentence makes it sound, but it was for me. I wouldn't learn the politics of friend-zoning until many years later from my daughter Rachel.

Yes, I can look back with humor and understanding, but at the time it hurt. From seeing LeeAnne's bike snuggled next to Marc's apartment onward, I wanted college to be over. I didn't know what I desired, but I knew I had to leave town.

During our trip to Tijuana, I experienced two tantalizing scenes. Marc's older brother lived in Los Angeles where he attended UCLA film school. We paid him a short visit to say a quick hello. He was working on a freshman year homework assignment, editing a short silent film on Super 8. He had a viewer and showed me his images as they flickered forward and backward on the screen at various speeds as he turned the hand cranks. He showed me how he'd determine where to make a cut and how to apply a splice. I wanted his apartment to be our destination. Driving through the heart of Los Angeles an hour later, we drove past a movie theater showing Fellini's *And the Ship Sails On.* I resisted the urge to have Marc pull over and let me out. I wanted to watch the movie and hitchhike back to his brother's place.

I was seeing puzzle pieces of my future, but the box lacked a picture to guide me. I was going to have to figure it out—trial and error—as I went along.

~paralyzing insomnia~

AS COLLEGE ended, I lived back at home with Mom. The time to take four years of college investment and cash it in on a career had arrived and I was already experiencing the wanderlust I imagine Dad felt before he "lost" his position at IBM. He'd lasted on the job for eighteen years. Was I going to find a job, so I could become bored, so I could "lose" it as well?

Mom found me floating in her condo complex's pool. I sipped from a bottle of Heineken, but no reggae played, and no friends hung out.

"Todd. What are you doing?"

"Well, I'm just drifting...here in the pool," I replied.

"Why?"

"Well, it's very comfortable just to drift here."

"Have you thought about getting a job?"

"No."

"Why did I spend all that money on college?"

"You got me."

Dad, during a rare visit, offered me one word of advice about my future. He whispered it in my ear: "Condos."

(And, yes, I'm riffing on scenes from *The Graduate*. But my God, I watch Dustin Hoffman in those scenes of post-college disarray and recognize how universal they are.)

Amid a bout of paralyzing insomnia, I cast out résumés. Zero bites. I reared back and cast farther. Stories of my fellow soon-to-be-grads landing jobs in Santa Barbara and nearby Lompoc poured in. I became depressed. I'd lie on the living room floor for hours staring at the ceiling while Mom worried.

"Todd, shouldn't you follow up with phone calls?"

"Oh God, Mom! No!"

Nudging me from my stasis, the phone rang—a call from

Seattle. Initech wanted to interview me.

I'd never flown anywhere before. I had to gather courage all week. A rental car awaited my arrival, already paid for; I told the desk clerk my name, he checked my driver's license, and handed me the keys. If I'd had to rent the thing myself from scratch, who knows? I might have never left the airport.

I trembled the entire time I drove from airport to hotel and hotel to interview and back to hotel again. (I did surprise myself—then and now—by venturing into the city to have a look around.)

During my interview, I sat and tried to swallow a sudden tidal wave of saliva threatening to drown me. I'd mailed them my original résumé copy with corrections, Wite-Out, and notes scribbled on the back. Those were typewriter and copy machine days. As I sat across the table from two Initech hiring managers, both named Bob, there it lurked in the middle of the table, taunting me. I expected them to ask me to explain my sloppiness. The only thing Bob asked, before his fellow Bob took me out for burgers and beer: "We have three positions. Which do you want?"

When I told Mom that I had been offered the job and planned to accept, she became silent for days. To me, it meant no more torturous interviews. To her, it meant the beginning of the end. When moving day arrived, I loaded bags and boxes into my inherited Toyota Corolla (I'd sold the VW Bug) while she stood in the carport sobbing. (Cheryl lived far away, off to college, her own transition into adulthood underway. On the way to Seattle, I spent a night at her apartment by UC Davis, meeting her roommates, finding them cute, afraid to talk to them, and trying to hide the huge zit sprouting out of the side of my nose.)

Writing about Mom's tears, I think about mine during her funeral. In preparation, I spent hours picking out photos for the service. I made two visits to the church to work with the A/V person to edit them into a slideshow. She and I watched the show twice, with Pachelbel's Canon in D and with a bit from one of Bach's Brandenburg Concertos. I chose the latter because I felt I could hear it and see those images without crying. During the service, one slide—of my mom as a nine-year-old girl—appeared and I sobbed as never before in my life. (In these pages, I'm describing almost every time I've ever cried. The times have been few but *have* become more plentiful with age.)

Moving and living far away in Seattle (and later North Dakota) meant she and I missed precious time together. Going through her belongings as I emptied out her condo, I learned she'd taken a class in watercolor painting. One of her works depicted a country road lined by a rail fence. The painting tilted the way her world did. She tended to see everything as if tipping over. Another painting showed a butterfly fluttering away. She knew how to make her art imitate her life.

Her crying as I prepared to run away toward distant Seattle also brings to mind my earliest vivid memory of the two of us. I was four, pissed off, and had gathered all I needed for a life on the road: my crocheted yellow blanket (which I passed on to both my daughters) and Ishy, my beloved stuffed animal fish. Ishy had seen better days. Gramma Dorothy had reluctantly but lovingly sewn him inside a tube sock to keep him from falling to pieces. She reassured me he slept tucked away inside a white sleeping bag. (Gramma Dorothy. Is she partly responsible for my obsession with *The Wizard of Oz*? She's Mom's mom—to me "Gramma Dirty" because once, while listening to her favorite radio talk show with Paul Harvey, she was chased atop the kitchen table by a mouse while shouting: "Dirty! Dirty! Dirty!")

What did I expect to find "on the road?" Without holding Mom's hand, I'd seldom traveled beyond "down the hall" to use the potty. Was I already sensing unhappiness between Mom and Dad and wanted to be anywhere else?

On the way out the door and with care, I'd wrapped Ishy in the blanket—a hobo's knapsack. The sidewalk felt cold on my bare feet and the chill rose all the way to my ass, covered by Snoopy pajamas. I'd walk the length of a house and turn around to see how far I'd traveled. Each time I did so, my house appeared a bit smaller, my troubles farther away. Each time, I turned and kept walking. I came to a cross street and the magnitude of my journey sank in. Crossing it would mean no turning back. I'd be on the road on my own forever. I checked inside my blanket for Ishy, making sure he hadn't fallen out. I looked back at my distant house, surely seeing it for the last time. I turned to face the street and with a tremble in my knee stepped off the curb—Sam taking his hesitant first step out of the Shire in *The Fellowship of the Ring.*

"Todd! Where are you?"

I turned to see a tiny version of Mom, leaning precariously on our distant front porch, supporting herself by a handrail, waving her free arm. (She'd probably been watching me the whole time.) As quickly as my tiny legs would carry me, I ran home and as I did, she grew back to full size until she enveloped me. As I pressed my face into the folds of her robe, I sighed. I could smell bacon on the soft fabric.

But at age twenty-two, I was leaving for good, and no amount of favorite breakfast food could keep me around. She waved goodbye.

The last box I loaded into the car felt heavy. I slid off the top and looked inside. It held my Super 8 movie camera and back issues of *American Film* magazine. I closed it again and placed it on the back seat, shut the door, hugged Mom, hopped in the car, and hit the road.

Once again, I felt I had all I needed.

SEATTLE

Back at my place, I played her a few short classical guitar selections.

~cheap rental furniture~

WHEN I'D visited Seattle for my initial-job-out-of-college interview, I'd learned four tidbits about the city: the location of the airport, that it had at least one hotel, how to find Initech, and there existed a cool place called the Guild 45th movie theater. I'm sure it comes as no surprise only the last one mattered to me. I'd been excited about my trip because *Amadeus*, which took forever to open in Santa Barbara, was playing in the city. It gave me the courage to leave my hotel room on the evening after my interview.

And after completing the long drive, I stood by my open car door in the parking lot of the one place I knew had warm beds, the Seattle Airport Marriott. I looked back and forth wondering what the hell one does in a strange city far from home. I've always pictured the scene in my mind from a low camera angle—me heroically framed against an enormous blue sky with a hint of clouds, a John Wayne in Monument Valley. I pulled a business card out of my wallet and found a pay phone. I dialed the number of one of two familiar voices in the city, the hiring manager who, after my interview, had taken me out for burgers and beer. He'd made the mistake of saying, "If there's ever anything you need, please call."

"Hi, Bob."

"Todd! Where are you?" he asked, sounding surprised.

"At a hotel. I thought I'd stay here until I find some place."

"Don't. It's too expensive. What number are you calling from?"

I read him the number from the pay phone. (Yes, this movie moment really happened in my life.)

"I'll call you back in a few minutes. Stay put," he said and hung up.

A half hour later, I drove toward an apartment complex in the hills east of Kent. He'd phoned ahead. When I walked into the office, a guy at the counter greeted me.

"You must be Todd! Welcome!"

Young, disheveled, and distracted as if he had been planning a day in front of the tube, he walked me through a second-floor, one-bedroom unit. I nodded my head and glanced from room to tiny room. My single question: "Where's the furniture?"

I'm amazed I didn't secure a second job as a mule for one of the drug dealers living in and operating out of the complex, but I felt happy. I had a place all to myself, soon to be filled with cheap rental furniture at exorbitant prices.

I DON'T remember my first day on the job at Initech, but I vividly remember my first trip as a resident into the big city. I'd been dying to see *Paris, Texas* ever since it won the Palme d'Or (grand prize) at the Cannes Film Festival. I scored a copy of the *Seattle Weekly* newspaper at the video store around the corner, flipped straight to the movie listings, and found it playing at the Harvard Exit. I drove to the Capitol Hill district of Seattle at my earliest opportunity—my second evening in town.

I'm a person who takes his seat in a theater before anyone else arrives, scrunches, interlaces his fingers behind his head, and daydreams, but as I neared the theater, my pulse raced. I saw nothing resembling a parking space in the whole damn city, just a bunch of cars parked closely in the streets. I glimpsed someone parallel parking. *The only way I'd slip in there is with Vaseline*, I worried.

Aunt Gwen would've empathized. Every time I drove with her in my car, she'd comment, "You're like me. We're both terrible backer-uppers."

I kept circling the block searching for a place to stash my Corolla and my heart sank. *Did I make this whole trip for nothing?* Out of the corner of my eye, I saw a parking lot with empty spaces. I ditched the car and made a mad dash for the theater.

The moment I crossed the threshold of the Harvard Exit, I recognized a perfect haven for cinema lovers: traffic-worn and homey foyer carpet, the ticket counter run by two men my age with beards and berets deep in conversation about the films of Wim Wenders (the German director of *Paris, Texas*). The poster for *Paris, Texas* on display had been imported from Italy. After purchasing my ticket, I strolled through the main lobby. It had a baby grand piano, its keys being tickled, impromptu, by a young female filmgoer.

Once the lights lowered, the movie swept me away. Ry Cooder's steel guitar strains and cinematographer Robby Müller's helicopter shots transform the opening desert setting into another planet. It could be John Carter's Mars, but who's the lanky, lonely, and lost man wandering through the landscape? There's nothing heroic about him. I'd long had a crush on actress Nastassja Kinski, who plays the movie's enigmatic lead. I hung a framed poster of her wrapped in a boa constrictor on my bedroom wall.

The climactic Sam Shepard dialogue—essentially a monologue—between Jane, played by Kinski, and Harry Dean Stanton's Travis through a two-way mirror in a house of kinky role-playing captivated me. Travis slowly reveals his identity to her by telling the story of how his young wife nearly burned him alive, and it ends with him fleeing into the night to eventually become that forlorn figure we met in the movie's desert opening. On the blind side of the two-way mirror, Jane uses few words, but it's Kinski's performance that tears me up. (And I mean "tears" both as in ripping up a piece of paper and as in salt water secreted from my eyes.) As she gradually recognizes the story is about him and her, she transforms from a sex worker into the estranged mother of his child—all through the shifting terrain of her facial expressions.

I was no longer watching a character named Travis. I saw myself (and Dad) trying to reconnect to some left behind someone. For one evening, at least, I moved beyond Luke Skywalker and—like a different Travis (Bickle) the prior year—tried an anti-hero on for size.

After the movie ended and I returned to Seattle, I left the theater behind and walked back to my car, in the dark, the wet sidewalks and streets shiny from streetlamps. As I turned the final corner and entered the parking lot, I saw a peculiar thing: a car crookedly parked, its front bumper touching my rear bumper. I let out a nervous laugh. I went to the door to unlock it and saw a sheet of paper beneath my wiper blade:

If you'd like us to set your car free, come to apartment 317.
We'll have you towed if we don't hear from you by 10:30.

My knees chattered so hard the two flights of stairs became the grand staircase in the Overlook Hotel in *The Shining*. I became little Danny. The room number may as well have been 237 and inside I'd find a rotting but still animated woman's corpse in a bathtub. I arrived at 317 and rang the bell.

The door opened immediately and before me stood a couple in their seventies. They reminded me of the old pair Holden Caulfield visits in *The Catcher in the Rye*, Mr. and Mrs. Spencer, after he's kicked out of Pencey Prep. I could smell Vicks VapoRub and see and hear a vaporizer running on an end table by the sofa. They relaxed when they looked at me, a nerdy, skinny, twenty-two-year-old.

"Son, I'm not going to come down on you too hard. Let this be a warning," the husband said. "We pay good money and one of our few niceties is returning home from being out and about and having a parking space waiting. Do you realize how you've put us out?"

I believe I nodded my head. His wife stood beside him caressing his elbow as if to soothe its arthritis.

"Look at me," he continued, "I'm still in my day clothes. I should be in my robe enjoying a second pipe and a chapter of *Moby Dick*. But look at me."

"Sorry," I said.

"Very well," he said.

His wife let go of his elbow and drifted into the kitchen. She returned holding a tray with a teapot, three cups, a bowl of sugar with a spoon, and a plate of coconut cookies.

"Are you hungry, young man?" she asked.

I should've been cautious—and would've been if I'd already seen *Rosemary's Baby*. (It's about a young couple drawn into a coven by an elderly couple.) They behaved too thrilled to have a pleasant young fellow over for the evening.

They eventually, and without inducting me into any form of devil worship, led me to the parking lot and set my captive car free. I wondered while driving home if they didn't intentionally leave their space open as a trap for unsuspecting young filmgoers.

A few years ago, I visited the Harvard Exit again to see the movie *Boyhood*. While waiting for the showing (once again, ridiculously early, but I'd been dropped off and didn't have to secure parking), I went for a walk. I wanted to revisit that apartment building and reminisce. And you know what? I couldn't find it. My mad dash must've been lengthier than I remembered.

A few months after seeing *Boyhood*, I heard the Harvard Exit itself had vanished. It would forever be reminiscence, its piano's keys sold and gently tickled elsewhere. (Every Seattle movie theater I mention in this memoir has fallen on hard times, I'm sad to say.)

AS I lived alone during my first year in my own tiny apartment doing little besides hoping David Lynch's *Dune* would be amazing (it was "interesting" and over-the-top grotesque and, as critic Robin Wood pointed out, homophobic—I prefer Denis Villeneuve's focus on the female characters), LeeAnne called. She'd opened her textbook, dialed my old number, and Mom had been happy to update her information.

"Hi, Todd."

"Hi…LeeAnne?"

"Yes. How've you been?"

"Good. What's up?"

"I'll be visiting Seattle for a wedding and was wondering if you know of places to stay and if you'd like to meet up sometime."

"I'd love to. When're you gonna be here?"

"In four weeks, for a few days."

"Hey, if you need a place to stay, you can use my bed and I'll take the couch."

"That might work," she said, her voice becoming a bit softer.

We arranged it. I'd have a houseguest for three nights in four weeks. My mind overflowed with possibilities. *Will this lead to something?* I wondered. Her mind read mine as well. A half hour later, she called again.

"Change of plans. I'm going to be staying with one of the bridesmaids."

"Okay. Let's still hang out."

"That'd be fun."

We never spoke again.

PARIS, TEXAS cast a spell over me, as did another indie film, *Stranger than Paradise*, a few weeks later. I unpacked and reread my *American Film* magazines, readied my Super 8 camera, imagining what I might do with it, purchased a splicer and hand-cranked viewer at a camera shop along with a few boxes of film, and started writing scripts—for real. The time had arrived for me to become a filmmaker and I produced crazy masterpieces in a frenzy of creativity.

To fill a void as a teenager, I'd purchased the camera, a basic and cheap Canon, at a neighbor's garage sale. My concept of an art movie with fancy dinners and faceless guests set on inescapable windy beaches hadn't yet materialized. College still in my future, Bergman, Fellini, and Buñuel still awaiting my discovery—and Suzie's bafflement—I rode my bike around Goleta after a rainstorm filming puddles and an abandoned shopping cart upturned in the middle of a vacant lot.

Memories of watching home movies with Grandpa Carl during summers spent in Oklahoma influenced me greatly. I remember him flipping the projector switch and hearing *clickety-clacking* followed by a scene of me as a toddler. Mom held me, feeding me. Dad sat next to her making faces for the camera. Grandma placed a platter of sandwiches in the center of the table. Dad grabbed one and munched away. Mom tried to as well, but juggling a tiny, wiggly child already required more than two hands. Grandma sashayed off-screen for a few moments to fetch a pitcher of lemonade and glasses which she filled. She disappeared again. Always serving and never sitting, a strict Southern Baptist, maybe she saved the good times for later.

"Do it backwards, Grandpa! Do it backwards!" I said.

He complied. He stopped the projector, flipped a switch,

and the reels reversed direction. We both laughed until our sides ached as Dad ate and drank in reverse and I screamed "Gross!" every time it made him appear to throw up.

With my camera in hand, I fantasized about my life being a movie. I could loop my life through a projector, watch it, and then run it backward. The images would flow back in time. I could have a do-over. Cinema is a time machine. *Through it I'll hold the door as Anny hops into my passenger seat*, I'd dream. Unfortunately, movies allow us to revisit the past, but the pictures are always the same every time we watch them.

As a young man in Seattle, I was ready to play life forward again. I found two coworkers who were game to play along: Paul and slightly older Conrad (Conny). We three hit it off. We all arrived from Southern California and Paul from UCSB. (We hadn't been acquainted, because I'd been watching everything directed by Federico Fellini while he learned Thermodynamics and Strength of Materials.)

Paul, blond, five feet eight and skinny, nerdy, and easygoing, couldn't wait to become acquainted with the nearby ski areas. He loved aviation and NASA history. We spent time talking about the scientific plausibility of *2001: A Space Odyssey*.

"Why isn't the Discovery One cool and streamlined?" I once asked. "It has this big, round head, a long spine-looking body, and a big butt."

"Todd. Outer space. It's a near-vacuum. It doesn't matter how it's shaped. It just needs to be functional," he said.

"Oh, yeah." I should've paid attention during physics.

I knew Conny was a guy to hang with when he flashed me his Playboy Club membership card the day we met. His PBR (Pretty Blond Radar) also intrigued me. One time, out driving, he pointed to a car ahead of us. We could see a head of long blond hair swaying behind the wheel.

"She's hot," he said.

"How can you tell? It's the back of her head. She might be old or have a hatchet face or even be a guy or something," I said.

"No, I can tell. She's hot."

I insisted on following the car for a closer look. I became a private investigator. I kept reminding him not to follow too closely, but not to lose her either.

The car pulled into, I couldn't believe my eyes, the parking lot of a Deja Vu strip club and drove around to the back. We followed her far enough to watch her park while maintaining a discreet distance. She sat in the car for several minutes, her head bouncing to unheard music on a Walkman like Nastassja Kinski's Jane in *Paris, Texas*. Her car door opened and out she stepped. She had Jessica Rabbit curves. With a flip of her hair, she turned toward us. Conny won. About twenty-one and a knock-out, she sauntered to the service entrance and the door closed behind her.

"What did I tell you?" he said.

"I'll never doubt you ever again."

He started to pull out of the parking lot, and I said, "Should we go in and try to meet her?"

To my relief, he said, "No. You can't meet the girls at these places unless you have a wallet stuffed full of twenties."

We took off.

He impressed me as a true man of the world, but not perfectly suave. A young woman named Jenny started working in our office. Young and cheerful, her laugh spread about the building every time she talked to someone which, given her job as administrative assistant, was all the time. I found Initech suffocating. I needed diversions and her presence helped speed the days along.

Conny had the eye for Jenny from day one. He'd walk past her to the coffee break room and restroom beyond her desk. He drank a lot of coffee and, therefore, had to pee a lot. She talked on the phone while swiveling in her chair with the cord wrapping around her.

One day, while walking toward the restroom, he eyed her as he walked past, and she stopped swiveling, looked into his eyes, and smiled. He kept his eyes on hers and ran right into a file cabinet, knocking it over, the crash heard around the building. Together, they righted the cabinet and restored the papers—previously piled atop the cabinet—that had been sent flittering everywhere. When he returned to his desk after making it to the restroom, he found a Post-it note with her phone number. Playboy Conny met his match.

They went out that night. The next morning, both sat at their desks looking bleary. He wore the same clothes, wrinkled. I wondered if he ran into the file cabinet on purpose. Locking eyes and file cabinets tumbling. Do we seize the moment or does the moment seize us? And how can we tell the difference? The moments are always happening right now; we experience—or sometimes survive—them, and only begin to sort them out in retrospect. That falling file cabinet is, now, a beautiful little moment in two people's lives. At the time, it was hopefully funny but mostly embarrassing.

MY FIRST movie production caused both Paul and Conny to doubt my sanity. No plot, just two men playing cards, guzzling beer (for real), and slithering around the floor of my apartment. The camera could take one frame at a time and I toyed with it. When they arrive at my apartment building, they don't walk up the stairs, they dart in sped-up fashion like a stop-motion scene from the Beatles' *A Hard Day's Night.* Cards aren't dealt. They pop into each player's hand. Beer is consumed so fast glasses empty without being lifted. Paul understood animation. He spent the day giggling.

After I wrapped the shoot, he stuck around for a while and told me about a condo opportunity.

"It's perfect. It's way down in Federal Way, but it's too nice to turn down. Two bedrooms. I need a roommate. You interested?"

"Does sound sweet," I said.

We checked out the condo the next afternoon after work. We moved in the following month. I returned the cheap rental furniture, but still had to pay two remaining months on the contract. I shrugged it off. *What's money?*

The audience response to my inebriated and reptilian movie—my living room, drunken laughter—encouraged me. Paul—my regular movie star by default—and I soon embarked on another production. One of his college buddies, Dragan, visited and we recruited him as well. (In a Facebook post, Dragan referred to the experience as his "fifteen minutes.")

The plot involved a poor soul, Paul, who came upon dark times after taunting a hitchhiker (my one acting role). Paul pretended to pull over to give me a ride but peeled out as I opened his car door. This led to mayhem, making no sense at all, and climaxed with a manic scene in the parking lot of our condo complex. I told Dragan to brandish a butcher knife and chase Paul. Paul fled in terror. As the director, I made two grave errors, one leading to the other.

We prepared to shoot the scene by drinking four beers each, something I doubt is allowed on professional sets. Dragan had the hilarious idea (I assure you it made us all laugh at the time) of dropping his pants around his ankles for the shot. Sloshed, my mind full of visions of Steve Martin's Navin R. Johnson from *The Jerk*, pants around his ankles and paddleball game in hand, I gave his improvisational idea of running in a precarious state of dress while wielding an eight-inch knife a thumbs-up.

The shoot started out well. I filmed from two angles. I ran with the camera, chasing Paul as he looked back in terror. The camera bounced and jiggled—perfect. I ran through the parking lot, pointing the camera back over my shoulder as Dragan chased me with the knife, the idea being to intercut the two shots. Overnight, I'd become cinematically sophisticated.

My angle on Dragan also went well, but before I yelled "Cut!" Dragan plummeted from my view. I stopped running and looked at him on the ground, laughing in a heap. Paul and I ran to check on him and he rolled over saying, "Good thing I fell on the handle."

I helped him to his feet, and he winced while still laughing. I called it a wrap and we all had another cold one. Dragan hit the road for home the next day. A few days later, he called and told Paul he had fractured a rib.

The movie took me several weeks to edit. In one leap, I'd gone from letting the three-minute roll of film play the way I'd shot it to shooting several rolls and cutting around eighty-five shots. I added animated titles and a musical score consisting of a painstakingly cued cassette tape with samples from my LPs, including "Draw the Brakes" by Scotty, "Teenager in Love" by Dion and the Belmonts, and "Always Look on the Bright Side of Life" by Monty Python. I released pause on the tape deck after flipping the projector switch.

I held the big premiere in the living room of our condo with a small gathering of friends. Everyone laughed and Jenny's younger sister, Enid, laughed the loudest. She and I made eye contact. I looked away. Shelly all over again.

~i didn't say anything~

WITH ENID, my education in adult relationships began. My first lesson: how to take no for an answer. Final grade: C-.

It took me two weeks to summon the courage to call Enid. She lived with Jenny and Conny, so I already had her number. I phoned from an unused office with the door closed. I knew she'd be home alone after school. Two rings, three rings, four rings. Another ring and I would've hung up.

"Hello?"

"Hello…Enid?" I had to swallow hard and catch my breath.

"Yes," she said.

"This is Todd. Remember me? I made that hitchhiker movie?"

"Yes," she said softly.

"I was wondering if you'd…go out with me."

Silence, long silence, unbearably long silence.

"I don't think so." *Click.*

I called her several times during the following days and she eventually said, "Todd, I like you, but I have problems you can't handle."

Unbelievably, I still called her one more time. I see my grade plummeting with each memory: D-.

JENNY, CONNY, Enid, Paul, and I decided to hold weekend movie nights. (Okay, Jenny, always the social organizer.) When it was Jenny and Conny's turn to host, and my turn to bring the movie, I saw Enid for the second time. I brought a movie sure to be a hit—funny, inventive, smart, and so damn cool. I wanted to share it with all my friends and have a happy time with beer and popcorn. *A Clockwork Orange.*

We settled in and watched Alex and his droogies (the movie's word for buddies) drink milk laced with drugs. The living room remained quiet, although Conny did smile. Alex beats an old drunkard in a shadowy tunnel, and I let out a chuckle while nobody else appreciated the humor. A rival gang attempts to rape a young woman on a theater stage. Enid moved to the edge of the couch, about to rise. Alex and his droogies pick a fight with the gang while the victim makes her getaway. Enid settled back onto the couch. The next scene where Alex and his droogies play "hogs of the road" (speeding in a sports car, they play chicken with oncoming vehicles) eased the tension. It *is* funny. And then the home invasion scene arrived.

Alex and Co. use a bit of trickery to gain access into the country home of a writer and his wife. The writer is subdued, gagged, and forced to watch Alex rape his wife. Adding to the already unsettling vibe is the way Alex sings "Singin' in the Rain" throughout. As this played out, Enid leaped to her feet and ran from the room in tears. I can still hear the slam of her bedroom door decades later.

I pressed pause, on the VCR and on the night. Jenny glanced at Conny and Paul. Conny went to the kitchen. Paul said, "I'm going to go take a leak."

Jenny studied me. A videotape-wavy image of Alex DeLarge remained frozen on the television screen. Ignoring Jenny's cautions, I did all I could think to do. I headed toward Enid's bedroom.

I tapped on her door, could hear muffled crying but no reply, knocked again and said, "Can I come in?" Still nothing. I lingered, treading in uncharted waters. I turned to go back to the living room and heard a faint, "Yes."

I turned the knob and went inside, closing the door partway behind me, and sat at the foot of her bed, keeping my distance. She had her face buried in her pillow, her tears easing.

"I'm so sorry," I said.

She didn't say anything. I didn't say anything else. *A Clockwork Orange* has been my least favorite Stanley Kubrick movie ever since. (What the hell? Why didn't I rent something like *Young Frankenstein*?)

My heart ached over what I'd done to Enid. Her role in my story could have ended, but one day, I can't remember how many days later, my phone rang.

"Would you go to Enid's prom?" Jenny asked.

I had never been to a single dance while in high school (as you know), and being asked to dance within the safety of a party at my own house had sent me scurrying to my bedroom. There was no Enchantment Under the Sea for me. The word "prom" filled me with fear.

"With her?" I asked.

"Sort of. Her friend Sharon needs a date. She's going with Conny's younger brother Bucky."

"Okay," I said, feeling relieved.

"Perfect," she said and hung up.

Ever since Conny started dating Jenny, Bucky had his eyes on Enid. He'd seen her in a photo and his phone calls to his older brother became frequent. "Jenny's sister is cute," I imagine he'd say. "Is she in a relationship? Would she go out with me if I flew to Seattle?"

"Give it a shot," Conny would likely reply.

Meanwhile, I needed to meet *my* potential date. Enid arranged a weekend lunch for the three of us. Sharon was warm, sweet, and funny; she repeatedly twirled her red hair with her thumb and index finger and, after releasing it, it performed a pirouette. It mesmerized me. *How does she not have an actual boyfriend?* I wondered.

During that lunch, I had nothing to say to either girl. They had nothing to say to me. They talked while I poked at my salad, watched Sharon's hair audition for the Bolshoi Ballet, and barely listened to their conversation. The date ended with Sharon somehow satisfied that she'd survive the dance with me as her date. The prom was a go.

A few days later, Bucky flew into town. He struck me as a kindred spirit, a nice, quiet, lonely, and funny guy. We had plenty of topics to discuss. He loved books and movies, and, for bonus points, had also seen *Paris, Texas*. We experienced an instant, mutual guy-crush, but sadly, we had little time to bond. With the big night two days away, haircuts and tuxes occupied our free hours.

The next step: meet Sharon's parents. I walked into her house, corsage in hand, and they stood side by side, arms crossed. They looked at me for a moment and all their worries departed. They let out a joint sigh of relief, uncrossed their arms, and all but offered me a drink. Was I so clean-cut parents would instantly trust me, an adult male, with their barely eighteen-year-old daughter? They laughed and kept reminding me not to keep her out too late after the dance. I remained politely quiet, my evening hampered by a sore throat. I placed flowers on Sharon's wrist, slipped her shawl over her bare back and shoulders, and posed for a few memory shots—of their daughter and a guy who exists for one page in their family album.

During dinner, the girls sat across the table from us guys, looking striking. They ordered pasta dishes. Sharon's had three shiny shrimp on top, glistening in a tomato sauce. Enid's had a white sauce with hints of green from peas and broccoli. Neither touched their plates. They nibbled from the bread basket. I *almost* dared to help myself to Sharon's shrimp. The girls "went to the bathroom" three times. Bucky and I talked about California.

After arriving at the dance, the girls mingled, leaving the two of us (or maybe just me) sitting alone eating chips and drinking transparent plastic cups of punch. I drank and wished I truly drank. The chips scraped past my tonsils. My "date" returned when she wanted a ride home.

The next day, Bucky caught a plane, and I began a course of penicillin for strep throat. Luckily for Sharon, we hadn't truly been a couple and hadn't kissed good night.

Just like a few short years before with LeeAnne, I did have a movie "date" with Enid. It was Jenny's idea, as I recall. We went to Francis Ford Coppola's *Gardens of Stone*. The movie is spiritless, perfunctory, cold, and depressing. My memory of the evening (or an afternoon?) paints it as my driving to a cruddy mall theater, my sitting mortified by what I saw on the screen, and my driving her home again. I don't recall a single word passing back and forth between us the entire time. (Am I imagining she tagged along?) Coppola had been tormented and shattered during the production of *Gardens*. His eldest son Gian-Carlo had died in a speedboating accident. I sure knew how to pick date movies.

I saw Enid on one other occasion, at her high school graduation open house. She appeared as happy as I ever saw her, and I gave her a gift of a set of dishes for the apartment she shared with two friends.

"You can make me dinner sometime," I said, still trying one last time to turn her no into a yes. (Maybe a D- was too generous.)

"That'll be hard to do. I joined the Navy and start basic in two weeks," she said.

She "boarded a bus" and disappeared like the character at the end of *Ghost World*. (Enid is a pseudonym inspired by that movie's protagonist played by Thora Birch. There are few if any movies I identify with as deeply. Steve Buscemi's character, Seymour, is like my alter ego. After you've finished reading this book, watch it sometime and keep an eye out for the references I've made to it—including referring to myself as a "doofus.")

The last time I thought about Enid was at a garage sale. My gift sat on a card table, pushed into a corner. The box had never been opened.

~everything on the menu~

AFTER MY brush with "romance," I needed to work out my frustration. Paul and I rented our condo from a law student and bodybuilder named Doug—rugged, chiseled, with muscles upon muscles, and a mild manner. He exuded hotness.

He noted our scrawniness and offered his assistance. After all, how were we going to secure dates without a major overhaul? We joined a health club, hit the weights, and soon muscles bulged, microscopically. We thought ourselves two Arnold Schwarzeneggers, until we gazed into the bathroom mirror before stepping into the shower.

One of the girls at the health club's front desk moonlighted as a Seahawks cheerleader, a Sea Gal. One afternoon, after swiping my membership card, I suggested we have dinner sometime. She smiled and laughed. I continued walking and took out my frustration on the bench press machine.

Paul and I played racquetball. We knocked our blue balls around a couple of days a week. I joined a league and took third place. I moved up a level and my opponents ran me in circles. Sulking, ready to abandon my new sport forever, I was rescued by Doug.

"I have an ex-girlfriend, Diane, who is an expert player. I'll see if she'll give you lessons," he said. He had lots of ex-girlfriends.

Two lessons with her and I wondered why Doug let her walk away. She was about three years older than I was, athletic, a short-haired brunette, fun to be around, and easy to talk to. Feeling bolder than ever before—because I'd spent an hour alone with her in the confines of a racquetball court—I wasted no time asking her to join me for an evening at the symphony, a classy move, I thought.

"Yes," she said. "Make sure to get three tickets."

"What do you mean?"

"I want my daughter to hear the symphony as well."

Surprised, I pressed on.

A few weeks later, the three of us went out to eat in Chinatown. Diane picked at her food, not into the exotic, while her eight-year-old daughter Kelsey and I had a blast trying everything on the menu.

"They have octopus," I said.

"Gross. Let's get it," Kelsey said, laughing.

I decided it would be fun to have kids. I fantasized about becoming her stepdad.

At the concert, an agreement they'd made prior to the evening—or an unspoken communication on the spot between mother and daughter—resulted in Diane and me sitting a seat apart with Kelsey between us. I wanted to sit next to my grown-up date, but I figured it would be fun to sit next to Kelsey and see if she enjoyed oboes and violas as well as squid and octopus. During the concert, I wanted to put my arm around Diane, but I could only stretch far enough to tickle her nearest shoulder. Kelsey became her date shield. She sat between her mom and me as Cheryl had once stood between Shelly and me. Was Kelsey protecting me from her mom—or her mom from me? In either case, I imagine the people seated behind us enjoyed plenty of extra entertainment for their dollar. Kelsey kept looking back and forth between her mom and me with an all-too-aware smile.

After the performance, of which I didn't hear a note, we walked to a place around the corner for pie and ice cream, then I drove them home. Oblivious to Diane's signals all night, I wondered if I should kiss her as I parked in front of their house. She spared me the awkward moment by bolting from the car and motioning for Kelsey to follow.

"Night," I said.

Diane forced a smile and said, "Good night." She walked away.

"Night. Thanks for the octopus," Kelsey said as she hopped out of the car, experienced at out-funning her mom on dates.

After our inauspicious night out, I called Diane again.

"I was wondering if you'd like to get together again," I said.

"Todd. Uh, I—"

"—don't think it's a good idea," I finished for her.

Another moment of silence and we both hung up.

A serious case of glumness settled in after my date with Diane. I consumed a few bottles of Jack Daniel's. I may have eaten food as well. I couldn't figure out what I'd done wrong. She'd been pleasant on the racquetball court. Did she hate Chinese food *that* much?

AUNT GWEN told me reading stories helps us understand people. I'm finding writing has helped me understand myself. Stories are about heroes going on adventures and transforming. Has the act of writing this book—and how the process has overlapped in time with Mom's final days—been my hero's journey? I don't feel I'm the same person as when I began writing it.

As I had with Enid, I made progress with Diane. I faced what I must've felt at the time to be certain rejection by calling her and asking her for a second date. I remember the tone of her voice betraying her effort to not crush me. I didn't call her again. I'd raised my grade to a B-.

Diane did Doug a favor. She hoped to take a step toward restarting a relationship with him. She'd agreed to help a shy, skinny guy improve his game—racquetball, that is. And I'd ruined it by trying to take it further. I thought, *Oh my. I may be a few dates away from never having to do this dating thing ever again. I could have a running start on a family and she's a sweet kid.* Did Diane see right through me, terrified by how fast my mind moved? Did she spend the night at the symphony cursing Doug for talking her into such a mess?

After my call to Diane, Paul poked his head into my bedroom. Had he been eavesdropping?

"I asked her out again and she said no," I said.

"Too bad." His look said he'd already read this page.

I did learn one new thing. I'd been rejected by two women (not counting the Sea Gal) and it hadn't killed me.

~Gounod's *Roméo et Juliette*~

I'D NEVER considered attending an opera with its bellowing people standing upon a stage, but watching *Amadeus* changed everything. It captivated me with the music and the characters accompanying the music. About a year after moving to the city, I saw my first live opera, *The Magic Flute*. I fell in love.

Playful and magical, it opens with a guy, Tamino, being threatened by a dragon. My love of Tolkien resurfaced. Tamino is rescued by three supernatural maidens. While he's passed out from fright, they all fight over who stays with him. When he awakens, they hand him a portrait of Pamina, and he sings a beautiful love aria. It tore my heart out.

It wasn't the hero Tamino who most affected me, but the earthy, lonely, and longing-for-love Papageno. He's such a fool. He's pathetic and clueless and I rooted for him as he searched for his Papagena. And when he found her, their duet about her becoming his darling wife and him becoming the dove of her heart left a smile on my face for days.

As Luke Skywalker had supplanted Tarzan as my teenage hero, Papageno took the baton during my early twenties. My desire for a girlfriend became operatic.

When a family member visited, I'd swap my one Seattle Opera ticket for two—or in one case, three. When Mom visited, we saw Gounod's *Roméo et Juliette*. For Cheryl, I snagged those three tickets for Verdi's *La Traviata*. I took my boss's daughter, Sylvia, as well. I had a crush on her. A year later, she married a lucky guy. As for Dad, I finagled a pair of tickets to Johann Strauss's *Die Fledermaus*. None of them had interest in opera, but Mom and Cheryl enjoyed it.

Dad refused to have anything to do with spending over three hours "listening to people screech in German." He found the whole idea of a flying mouse ridiculous. He insisted I instead drive him through the swankiest neighborhoods of the city. He spent the whole evening daydreaming out loud about moving his real estate life to the Pacific Northwest.

Mom—although it was a major undertaking for her to walk the required distances—went out with me to an Irish pub followed by a movie at the Seven Gables Theater, a place as cozy as her living room. We saw *Madame Sousatzka* with Shirley MacLaine, her choice and a pleasant one. Back at my place, I played her a few short classical guitar selections. ("Few" and "short" are the operative words. My time spent practicing: still paltry.)

When Dad visited, by nighttime he complained about being tired. He wanted to stay in and watch one of my videotapes. I showed him my collection. Nothing appealed to him and we watched television.

On the last day of his visit, he sat looking across the room at my CDs and a boxed set of Mozart piano concertos caught his eye.

"I love piano music. That'd make a nice Christmas gift," he said.

He hit the road back to California.

Planning to fly his way for Christmas, I went to Tower Records a few days later and spent hours selecting a collection of classical piano CDs, a handsome handful of a half dozen. I gift-wrapped them and set them aside, ready for my flight in December.

Having divorced parents living three hours apart turned vacation visits into emotional tugs-of-war. I'd spend most of my time with Mom and a few hours with Dad.

That year, Cheryl and I spent Christmas Eve with him. We did our gift exchanging in the afternoon and I couldn't wait to give him his CDs. I hoped to stay a bit longer than planned so we could listen to one, a recording of Grieg's Piano Concerto in A minor performed by Philippe Entremont. He'd owned the recording on LP, and I'd often listened to it. Dad tore the wrapping paper from the box and tossed it aside. He opened the box and shuffled through the CDs with his fingers.

"I was hoping you'd get me the boxed set *you* have." He set them aside and reached for another package to open.

We stuck to our original plans and drove down the coast to Mom's condo an hour later. I couldn't listen to Grieg for years. Happily, when I did again, he had lost none of his charm.

I came across letters in Mom's antique, fold-down desk while cleaning it out. They included an exchange, through attorneys, in which Dad pleaded with Mom to relieve him of his $350 per month alimony obligation.

Mom, worrying about the possibility of being laid off, wrote, "I do not know what the effect of my cerebral palsy will be on my getting other work: it seems reasonable to me, however, to believe both my age and my cerebral palsy are going to be impediments."

Dad replied, "I am sorry Beverly has a handicap. I did not cause the handicap. She had it before I came along. I have financially supported her (all or in part) for 32 years. I think I have been punished long enough for a bad marriage."

Dad's marital difficulties involved one thing—Mom's cerebral palsy. His comment about not causing it and her having it before he came along says everything. *Of course, she had it before you came along. What went through your mind when the two of you dated? Isn't that something you and your girlfriend should've talked about before buying a ring?*

Before I become too hypocritical, I too had a hard time dealing with the way Mom walked. After arriving in DC during our 1975 vacation trip, we visited the Smithsonian Institute. Talk about a giant museum. It's big enough for a family to wander lost in for days. Most museums whittle the world down to something bite-size such as antique cars, comic books, or flora of the Southwest, but the Smithsonian thwarts the schedules of vacationing families with but a single day to spend and we had a mere four hours. We needed to be blinkingly fast. But we walked at Mom's speed, always too slow for Dad—and for me. We saw a sliver of the museum. I'd stray as far ahead of my family as I could, once ducking into a room filled with gold coins, leaving the slow-moving trio far behind.

If someone asked me as a kid what superpower I most wished to possess, I'd always answer, "Invisibility." Because of her cerebral palsy, which caused her feet to drag and scrape across the floor, drawing all ears and then eyes in her direction, being with Mom was the opposite of being invisible.

During a day in the third grade when parents took turns visiting my classroom, I nervously sat at my desk in the front row. Mom walked in, sat in a tiny chair in the back of the room, and smiled at me. I glanced at classmates as they looked at me and at her and back at me and I jumped from my seat and ran from the classroom, leaving a trail of vomit in my wake. I don't remember feeling nauseated. One moment, I sat in my chair. The next, I lost my breakfast. My body must've decided it was as good a way as any to escape.

"Todd!" Mom screamed. I heard her tiny chair tip over.

She moved as fast as she could from the classroom, following my trail to the boys' bathroom, and, to my embarrassment, right on inside she came. I don't know what I would have done if there had been other boys in there. Once I'd finished puking, she dragged me to the office, signed me out, and took me home to spend the afternoon lying in bed on towels, nostrils filled with Lysol.

That evening, I stood before her and mumbled, "Mom, I don't think you should come to my school anymore."

She looked at me, wounded.

"You don't like the other kids seeing how I walk?" she asked.

"Yes," I said, relieved, thinking she understood completely.

I turned to walk away. After taking a few steps, I looked back to see her in tears.

"Get out of here," she said.

I did. It was one of those moments where you say something and spend the rest of your life wishing you could take the words back.

(I was eight years old. I was five when I smiled and kissed my babysitter's daughter. I was eleven when I couldn't look

Shelly in the eyes and my lips wouldn't cooperate. Might this have been what happened in between? I'd opened my mouth and out came a horrible utterance. Ever since, I've had a propensity to talk to myself, to test my words before trusting them and seldom feeling satisfied.)

Throughout my life and especially during my adult years, I remember Mom falling—a lot. And she'd always be angry with herself—and with me if I tried to help her to her feet. One time, she fell by our car in the parking lot of the Elephant Bar restaurant in Goleta. Using a walker with wheels, she failed to squeeze the handbrakes and it rolled away from her. She had no strength in her lower body. Left to her own, she would've had to crawl to the car and sit until someone happened by to her rescue. I instinctively lifted her back onto her feet. She weighed not over one hundred pounds. But my assistance angered her.

"Todd! Stop it! Let me do it!"

"But I got it, Mom."

"Todd! No!"

A group of evening-dressed young women came out of the restaurant, falling-over drunk. They didn't stop walking and ignored our predicament. After they passed us, we heard laughter. Mom remained silent the rest of the evening. Her silence brought and still brings back memories of my asking her to no longer visit my school. I'd realized Dad's worst fears.

As I look back through shoeboxes of photos (I gave up on photo albums long ago), her progression from standing with a slight tilt to balancing on a cane to leaning into a walker to frowning in a wheelchair tells a tale of growing frustration. Those pictures are hard for me to look at and I missed what she went through daily during the gaps between those photos.

As her health failed in her eighties, I moved her belongings into a storage unit by day and visited her in the mornings and evenings. She felt ill. She had a nasty, wet cough, once coughing so violently she kicked over her food tray. She tearfully apologized as I cleaned the mess. She had no energy. I had to do everything for her. To move her from her bed to the bathroom, I positioned her wheelchair by the bed, guided her as she transitioned from sitting on the bed to sitting on the chair, rolled the chair into the bathroom until it reached the toilet, and stepped out. I stood outside the door and worried. Would she make it from chair to toilet and back again? I listened for falling sounds.

"Todd. Todd."

I opened the door, and she awaited her return to bed. The dining room, a mere hundred feet away, may as well have been miles without my help. She overcame the hurdles of climbing in and out of my rental car to visit the condo, one last time. We ate at her favorite Mexican restaurant, one last time. We journeyed to church on Sunday. She never missed a chance to greet.

To cover distances beyond the confines of her apartment, her wheelchair needed to be outfitted with footrests. If not used, her feet would dangle close to the ground and risk dragging, folding under the chair, sending her toppling. The routine of attaching and removing those footrests became a source of pride for me. I insisted on them when—especially when—she told me not to bother.

"We aren't going far, Todd."

The motions of positioning the supports on pegs, lifting her feet (something her muscles had long been incapable of doing), swinging the supports into place, and lowering her feet onto them became so practiced my hands could perform the actions without looking.

But her cough, a nagging, unceasing cough she blamed on Mucinex, and her weaker than usual body were harbingers. I overlooked the strangeness of her having purchased larger shoes because the old ones "shrank." She had difficulty sleeping, but so do I, often.

Just weeks later, Cheryl messaged me saying Mom was hospitalized and dying. Time to regain lost time ran out. I wish I'd told her it meant the Universe to me that her expensively-glass-framed poster from Gounod's *Roméo et Juliette* never left its prominent location on her wall.

~i imagined our future~

ONE SUNDAY, I visited Conny and Jenny for lunch. A strange feeling permeated the air, as if they had something on their minds. Conny turned toward me. With Jenny beaming behind him, he asked me to be a groomsman.

Jenny, stepping forward, said, "One of my oldest and dearest friends from college, Monica, just has to be included. I can't believe I forgot about her until now."

"Sure, why not?" I said.

Paul and I threw Conny a bachelor party with the usual booze, junk food, and a surprise. A few hours before the party, Paul spilled the beans. He'd hired a stripper. When she walked into our condo, I caught a glimpse of the back of her head and her blond ponytail as she darted straight for the bathroom to adjust her hair and wiggle into her costume. My mind returned to the girl detected by Conny's PBR over a year prior. Was I about to meet her? A few minutes later she emerged from the darkened hall and danced into our living room. She had wrinkles, too few curves. Oh well.

Our party had turned decadent. Well, decadent by the standards of a few clean-cut enginerds anyway, a small step beyond the apartment of *The Big Bang Theory*'s Sheldon and Leonard. (And speaking of Sheldon and Leonard, they are named after Sheldon Leonard, the geeky, bow-tie-wearing director of episodes of *My Favorite Martian* and *Abbott and Costello Meet the Invisible Man*. I must be akin to Sheldon and Leonard. I can't believe I'm inserting this comment, interrupting a scene with a stripper.)

Wearing nothing but a thong and using it to collect money, our visitor writhed in our laps. When she sat facing me, I gave her tits a kiss. They felt rough. They disappointed me. They smelled of sweat and tobacco.

"You're a bad boy. No touchy-feely," she scolded.

Jenny later caught word of our night of debauchery and wasn't pleased, with us or with Conny. We feared she might be pissed off enough to cancel the wedding. Her maid-of-honor/eldest sister threw a bachelorette party, details of which barely reached my ears.

I first laid eyes on Monica the day of the wedding rehearsal and within seconds I'd planned *our* wedding. Timid, quiet, and with long, flowing blond hair, she redefined feminine loveliness. I imagined our future as an idyllic paradise, sharing a perfect and tiny house with a couple of kids dragging blankets behind them. By the time our turn came to practice joining arms and strolling out of the sanctuary, I'd forgotten all about Conny and Jenny. I had a lightness of step I'd never experienced before. Outside the sanctuary, I turned to Monica and said, "Let's do it again."

"No, I think we got it," she said, blushing.

During the ceremony, I admired the beauty all around me. Jenny had done a marvelous job of designing the dresses for the ladies of her court. Bare backs, low fronts, accentuating the women's curves or, in Monica's case, a sleek, slender, feline figure. Shiny red fabric flowed down their legs, teasing my fertile imagination.

The bright fabric of Monica's dress captured my eyes and refused to set them free, something she noticed—with embarrassment. She made tiny gestures as if trying to hide within the revealing dress. She'd tug on the fabric to cover her arms and lower legs and she turned her exposed back away from me with an awkward smile each time she caught me looking.

When our big moment came during the wedding—the time for me to walk toward her, take her by the arm, and stroll out into the world—I wished a soon-to-be-decorated car waited outside to whisk *us* away. Jenny had worked it all out and matched all the women of her court with "appropriate" guys. She would have considered it perfect if her coordination led to four additional weddings.

During the reception, champagne flowed. We gentlemen

and ladies of the court lounged around a table, Conny semi-conscious, Jenny bubbly and smiling at me drunkenly. Embarrassed, I looked away and locked eyes with Monica, who looked equally embarrassed, our initial private moment.

The DJ returned. I asked Monica to dance, and she let me lead her away without hesitation. During the fast songs, I moved spastically. For the slow ones, I wrapped my arms around her, our slow dancing becoming slow hugging, something I'd long wanted to try. She didn't resist, content to dance only with me—heavenly, but odd. It felt summertime warm in the room, but she had slipped on a dull brown, long-sleeved sweater covering her revealing bright red dress. No skin remained exposed; she'd morphed into a different person, full of confidence instead of self-consciousness. I loved how she felt in my arms but longed to feel her skin against mine. I luxuriated in her undivided attention all evening.

A few days later, back at the office, my immediate boss, who had been at the reception, said, "I saw a different you the other night. You were having fun all over the dance floor with that pretty young lady."

I'd spent the entire evening with my head in the clouds.

~she'd aimed for my cheek~

CONNY AND Jenny had a whirlwind honeymoon—in Tahiti? It lasted an eternity. I'd wanted to talk with Jenny about Monica the entire time. I needed advice. I finally got a chance to ask, "Do you think she would go out with me?"

"Why don't you find out, silly? Give her a call."

"I don't know her number. I don't even know her last name."

"Jesus, Todd. Do I have to do everything?" She wrote something on a Post-it note. "Do I need to call her for you, too?"

I shook my head and walked back to my desk, where I sat and read the note over and over for the remaining seven and a half hours of the workday.

As soon as I closed and locked our condo's door and stood by the kitchen counter, I dialed the number.

"Hi, Monica?"

"Yes."

"This is Todd. I've been wanting to ask you out ever since the wedding. Would you like to go out…with me?" I lost my breath for a moment.

Her initial quiet non-response worried me.

"Monica, are you okay?"

My question reassured her. "I'd love to," she replied.

Two days later, as I drove to a movie theater, I kept glancing at her.

"Eyes on the road," she kept saying.

She wore minimal makeup, jeans, and a T-shirt. She looked comfortable—with herself and with me. It didn't feel like a first date. It felt relaxed. I joked. She laughed.

We saw *Little Shop of Horrors* with Steve Martin at the Guild

45th Theater, a cozy, nondescript art house in northern Seattle near Ballard, and she squeezed my arm the whole time.

I remember Steve Martin's sadistic dentist. He sings of taking pleasure in inflicting pain and smashes an elderly dental assistant in the face with a door.

I wrapped my arm around Monica's waist as we left the theater.

"I enjoyed it so much," I said.

"Me too," she said.

"I'll watch anything with Steve Martin."

"I know. He's so funny."

I wanted to kiss her as we stood on a street corner waiting for the crossing light to turn green, but I didn't. I'm not sure what stopped me. Was I afraid I might ruin everything if I took it too fast? Was I afraid of being a bad kisser? Yes, and yes. I hadn't kissed a girl since my five-year-old experiences. I stood waiting for the light to change, glancing at Monica as if red light turning green meant "go for it." I didn't act quickly enough. She strolled across the street, pulling me along by the hand, the moment the opposing green light turned yellow.

Her soft sighs and thankful smiles punctuated our drive back to her house. I would become accustomed to driving her everywhere. She had a license, but no desire to use it. Seattle driving terrified her. She relied on buses and the kindness of others.

Pulling into her driveway, my thoughts focused on my surprise. I'd bought a tiny box of chocolates and had it tucked behind the driver's seat. When I put the car in park, I sensed the candy would be useful.

"I had a nice time," I said.

"Me too," she said.

We sat in silence for a moment. I've never had a talent for saying goodbye. Why are people expected to say anything? Why doesn't saying nothing imply "to be continued?" She reached for the door handle.

"Wait," I said, "I have something for you." I reached behind the seat and produced the tiny, wrapped box. She looked surprised, a blushing girl. "I really like you," I continued.

She took the box and leaned toward me to give me a quick kiss on the cheek, but I couldn't wait any longer. I turned toward her at the last moment and our lips met in a short semi-kiss. I quickly kissed her again, making it last. It felt and tasted as I remembered. It had the sweetness of Grampa Fred's peach. My heart pounded into my throat. Neither of us said anything else. She stepped out of my car and I watched her stroll into the house. I drove home without the tires ever touching pavement.

She'd aimed for my cheek. I'd moved the target once her lips took flight. And just like that, we became a couple.

ELATED, I called Mom the next day. She was *the* person I wanted to share my experience with. I wanted to reassure her she no longer needed to worry about never having grandkids.

"I met a girl," I announced. "I think I'm in love." (I must've sounded just like Mark Ratner in *Fast Times at Ridgemont High*, telling his friend Damone that he was in love after watching Stacy from across the room in biology class.)

"What's her name?"

"Monica."

"We were going to name *you* Monica if you'd been a girl."

"I didn't know that." (That admission makes me sad now. Did I talk to my parents at all?)

"Tell me about her."

"I met her at Conny and Jenny's wedding. She was a bridesmaid, and I was her groomsman. She's so pretty. She's been all I can think about ever since I met her."

"You didn't know her before?"

"No. I met her at the rehearsal, the wedding, and last night. I've seen her three times."

"It sounds like you had a nice date. What did you do?"

"We went to a movie."

"What movie?"

"We saw *Little Shop of Horrors*. It was funny and had Steve Martin as a crazy dentist and a giant carnivorous plant. It's a musical."

"Sounds interesting."

"I don't think you'd like it. But Monica loved it. She laughed and squeezed my arm the whole time. I didn't want it to end."

"What else did you do?"

"We walked back to my car and I drove her home and we kissed good night. Twice."

"You didn't go out for dinner or dessert?"

"No."

"Did you sit in the car and talk?"

"No. Why?"

She became quiet, my second awkward silence in two days.

"Todd. I want to tell you one thing about dating. Take your time. Talk. Make sure there isn't anything about her you don't like."

~everything to the imagination~

ONE EVENING, Monica and I were running barely on time to catch a dinner reservation and our journey took us into parts of the city neither of us knew well. In one of her happy moods, wearing a halter top and shorts, she sat as close to me as possible without interfering with the gear shift of my Honda CRX. (Both my life and my car had become sexier.) Every time she laughed, I could feel, smell, and taste her warm, sweet breath. We came to an intersection and I had to decide whether to go left or go right. I could see the lights of the restaurant straight ahead, dimly in the distance. I turned on the blinkers.

"No. Turn right," she said.

I switched the blinkers and followed her instruction. Within two blocks, it became obvious we were going to be in my car for a long time, trapped, headed across a floating bridge, during rush hour, slowing to a crawl, with no way out except to continue across Lake Washington, turn around, and come back. In the rearview mirror, I watched the restaurant lights recede. We were going to be hopelessly late for dinner.

I looked over to see her sobbing, shaking. "I'm sorry. I'm so stupid," she kept repeating.

"Don't cry. I didn't know where to go either," I said.

I turned up the music, smiled, and held her hand. She relaxed and laid her head on my shoulder as we crawled across the bridge. She kissed my cheek.

"I love being with you, anywhere with you, Monica," I said, "because I love you." She gave me another quick kiss and glanced out her window.

When we arrived at the restaurant, one parking space remained, in the rear by the staff entrance. I took it. There was a line out the door, and I asked with a glance if she still wanted to go in and eat. She answered by moving toward me until our lips met. I shut off the engine, slid my seat back to the last notch, and she finished hopping into my lap, all without our lips parting.

I placed my hand on her stomach and she said, "Not yet."

"Why not?"

"People should get married first," she said.

I didn't say anything.

"Todd, what do *you* think?"

"It's good to wait."

We kept kissing. Eventually, we heard laughter and glimpsed a couple walking by through our fogged over windows. We returned to our senses. Monica slid back into her seat and I drove her home.

On another date, we strolled along the shores of Green Lake and I let her pull ahead of me. I gazed at her and she turned around and caught me in the act.

"I can't believe you're looking at my behind," she said, her anger catching me off guard.

"I wasn't," I half lied. I'd been imagining how she looked beneath the concealing layers upon layers of heavy grey wool, a dress leaving everything to the imagination—on a warm afternoon.

I walked alongside her. Neither of us said anything for a while. As if sensing my hurt feelings, she moved to give me a kiss. I ducked. Not because I didn't want to kiss her, I usually did, but because our one kiss of the date prior to our walk had the bitterness of the peach I once found in the grass beneath Grampa Fred's backyard tree.

"Now what's wrong?!"

"Your breath stinks."

Monica became almost the angriest she'd ever be with me. She berated me for not telling her about her breath right away. We raced straight back to my car. She won.

"I hated that shopping for horrors movie," she said. "I hate Steve Martin!"

I didn't wait to watch her hurry inside her house. I swung by a liquor store, bought a sixer, and spent the evening watching zombies stagger through a shopping mall.

I feared she might break up with me, but the next time I saw her, she'd reverted to her happy self again, sweet breath and all. We spent another evening parked in my car, on the waterfront, once again omitting our planned dining. The windows fogged over, again. An occasional passing car slowed to rubberneck and honk.

Not all went well inside my car. Her "ex-boyfriend," I'll call him The Prick, had returned to Seattle for a visit during a break from law school. I wish I'd had warning, so I could've prepared myself for the brick The Prick dropped on my head from a rooftop.

"He's going to be in town for a week," she said between kisses.

"What?"

"Let's not see each other while he's here. He and I went out for a long time and I owe it to him."

"Are you going to tell him about us?"

"Yes."

I struggled for words. Before I could say anything further, she blocked my tongue with hers. (I'd left my high school Tarzan kissing fantasies long behind. I was ready for tongues.)

For the entire week of The Prick, I promised to give her space—she assured me—to say her goodbyes. And away I stayed.

This was 1986, the year of Steve Martin's sadistic dentist, *and* Dennis Hopper's more memorable creation, Frank Booth, a beyond sadistic whatever-he-is. *Blue Velvet* entered my dreams as I dated Monica, and the scenes foremost in my mind were the ones where Laura Dern's Sandy doesn't want her boyfriend, Mike, to know she's also dating (or sleuthing with) Kyle MacLachlan's Jeffrey. She still "loves" Mike and doesn't want her secret relationship with Jeffrey to be discovered. (Okay, I'll fess-up. The Prick's real name: Michael.)

I didn't call her. Inspired by *Blue Velvet*, I thought about stalking them. On his last evening in town, I knocked unannounced.

"Todd, what are you doing?! He'll be here any minute."

I walked past her and into the living room. Her parents weren't home. They would soon have the place all to themselves. I'd never had the place alone with her, not once, during the couple of months I'd known her. And she wore an apron. She'd never cooked for me. It smelled delicious, something Italian with onions, garlic, and olive oil. An open bottle of cabernet sauvignon breathed on the dining table between two place settings and beside a bowl of bread sticks.

"What are you making?" I asked while sitting on the couch.

She said, while sitting beside me, "Scaloppini. Yes, I know I told you I hate veal, but it's his favorite."

Before she could say another word, I did something I had never done in my life, something I found profoundly embarrassing. I sobbed uncontrollably. I laid my head in her lap and she stroked my hair.

"I'm sorry. I'm sorry. I'm sorry," she kept repeating.

She waited for me to calm down and I looked at her flipped upside-down face, distorted through my tears. I don't know what I expected to see, but what I saw…nothing.

"You should leave. I wanted to get through all of this without you two meeting," she said.

I left. I loved her. I felt her slipping away. Doing what she asked was, I thought, my only means of keeping her. I pulled to the side of the road halfway home and just sat there, watching cars pass me by.

~holding her breath her whole life~

MICHAEL WENT back to school the next day as planned and, as she'd promised, we went out (or, rather, stayed in).

"Did you tell him about me?"

"Yes."

"What'd he say?"

"I'll tell you later." (She never did.)

I felt I needed to make the night special—to compete with the evening she and Michael had the night before. I boiled spaghetti and heated Ragù. Filled a bowl with torn-up iceberg lettuce. Unscrewed the cap from a bottle of red wine the liquor store guy said would go with anything. I set the table (after first spending twenty minutes clearing it and locating Paul's place mats). I toasted and cut bread slices into strips because I'd forgotten bread sticks. Could my flimsy repetition have been more obvious? I kicked Paul out for the evening.

Monica's attire encouraged me. She wore shorts, once again a halter top, and, intriguingly, had no bra straps showing. Inside my front door, with the door still ajar, I held her for a long moment, enjoying the feel of her skin as I caressed the small of her back. We kissed, and her breath tasted delicious. She didn't resist my attentions. She encouraged them. *It's going to be all right*, I felt.

"Where's Paul?"

"He's with his girlfriend," I said. "We won't be seeing him tonight."

"Good."

In the kitchen, as I stirred the sauce and offered her a taste, she pressed behind me and wrapped her arms around my waist. She kissed my ear and blew against it—and we hadn't poured the wine yet. The evening wrote itself better than anything I could have scripted. *I should kick Paul out forever*, I thought.

After dinner, I put on Stan Getz's *Jazz Samba*, one of my favorites, and we curled together on the couch. One thing led to the next as smoothly as the music. One strap of her halter top slid from her shoulder right on cue and dangled. The Monica of my prior experience would've spent the evening pushing it back onto her shoulder. Hell, she wouldn't have worn such a flimsy thing at all, but not *that* night's Monica. She allowed her top to fall from her shoulder, exposing her left nipple without a care in the world.

And it happened. Her top kept falling as she made herself comfortable before me on the couch. Her breasts looked as beautiful as I'd imagined, and I'd imagined them often. I couldn't believe my eyes. I leaned forward and took a nipple into my mouth. Its softness erased the disappointing memory of the stripper. I started to give her a kiss, but I stopped, cold, and moved away from her. On her face, I didn't see the pleasure I expected. I saw a terrified expression. She trembled. She looked about to be sick. I took her top in my fingers and lifted it back onto her shoulders. I held her.

"I'm sorry," I said, and hearing those words she exhaled a sigh of relief as if she'd been holding her breath her whole life.

WORRY MINGLED with excitement in Jenny's voice when I phoned her and asked her to help me pick out an engagement ring for Monica, but once we hit the jewelry stores, she slipped right into the role of love accomplice. I had lots of money and my sights set on half carat at least, something Jenny ate up. She whistled her favorite song, "Shine on You Crazy Diamond" by Pink Floyd, throughout the mall. She picked out the biggest, most sparkly, most—

Okay, I'll stop. I know your mind is already pages ahead anyway. Soon, I'll be crawling to a jewelry store and begging for my money back. What was I thinking? Was I temporarily insane, blinded by love—or lust? No, something like rational thought must have been mixed in as well.

As IF I'd been playing a game of "She loves me/She loves me not," a coding bug stuck me on "She loves me." It's easily done. When I first learned to write JavaScript, I often made a common mistake. If you write

IF (HerStateOfMind = "She loves me") THEN

you haven't asked something the program will evaluate as TRUE or FALSE. You've accidentally instructed the program to set her state of mind to be "She loves me" forever. To check her state of mind, write

IF (HerStateOfMind == "She loves me") THEN

That one overlooked equal sign makes all the difference. Programming—like life—can be most unforgiving.

I hadn't yet learned heart-to-heart talks. I could have arrived at the same ending with Monica gracefully, less embarrassingly by talking with her, but I set the Fates in motion when I lied to her about sex. I didn't want to wait until marriage. I had wanted to sleep with her since the day I met her.

Sometime later, Jenny told me it was fortunate Monica and I never did have sex. She feared if she had become pregnant—or even if she hadn't—she might have ended it all.

Monica and I had been dating for three months. We hadn't talked seriously about anything. (Pop quiz: does our lack of communication remind you of anyone?) We certainly hadn't talked about marriage. With my back to the wall, I communicated everything at once. I don't think buying a ring and playing out the scene I'm about to narrate had anything to do with love, or lust. I dished Monica an ultimatum, my way of forcing her to choose between Michael and me. My grade in Dating 101 had plummeted: F.

Decades later, I think about these events and realize I'd been hopelessly unable to understand what was happening to me. I felt like Steve Martin's Rigby Reardon in *Dead Men Don't Wear Plaid* as Rachel Ward's Juliet repeatedly sucks bullets out of his shoulder to ease his pain—bullets from a gun she herself had repeatedly fired. One minute, Monica wanted me. The next, she didn't. I tried to make the times when she did want me last forever. I ignored all else. She was in love, to be sure, but not with me. She missed the man she did love, and I, a nice guy, conveniently placed to fill her loneliness, was what she needed, if I didn't try to take the relationship too far. If I didn't say, "I love you." Those last three sentences make it all sound so obvious when staring me in the face, so baldly from this page. Why wasn't it apparent in the moment?

The proposal began as all my dates with Monica had, with a long and lonely drive to her house. Both anxious and nervous, I couldn't see beyond that day. I went through the motions while not knowing whether the experience carried me toward dark clouds or clear skies.

After being greeted by her parents (who liked me), we hopped into my car and sped away. I had it all worked out and stage one went swimmingly. She displayed one of her pleasant moods. (Would I have aborted my program if she hadn't?) I thrilled her when I pulled into the parking lot of a cozy, romantic French restaurant. We were both French food virgins.

We sat at a table for two and held hands, illuminated by a single candle. We laughed as we realized neither of us could understand a single word on the menu. She held one hand over her mouth and one over mine to muffle the mirth. When the waiter came, we pointed at our menus and hoped for the best. The food tasted delicious, and I didn't flinch when the check arrived, and it was over $200.

Paul spent all his nights at his girlfriend's house by then. Monica and I settled into my living room. As if trying to avoid uncomfortable memories, we didn't move to the couch. Instead, I asked her to choose a CD while I built a fire. She picked *Jazz Samba* all over again.

I kept telling her we'd have a fun evening playing a game. She became little-girlishly curious. I motioned for her to join me on a blanket I'd spread before the fireplace. I kissed her while sliding my hand into my pocket. I wanted the first image she saw when our lips parted to be the sparkle of the diamond and I had to make the kiss last until we nearly passed out. The ring kept snagging in my pocket as if it felt ashamed.

Once I held the ring in my hand, I parted our lips and took a breath. I looked at her face and her closed eyes.

"Monica," I said softly.

She opened her eyes and I guided them downward with a glance. I looked at the ring in my hand as it sparkled by the light of the fire and imagined her reaction, trying to put ideas into her head. I looked at her face.

Tears flowed, and not joyful tears, not happy tears, not sad tears, but tears of anger. (Whenever I hear Stan Getz's "Samba Triste" to this day, my mood changes. It must've been the soundtrack for this pivotal moment.)

"Why are you doing this?" she asked.

"Because I love you and want to be with you always," I said, in an embarrassing series of clichés.

"But why me? Why?"

She had me stumped.

"Please, try it on," I said.

She gave me a glimmer of hope when she held out her hand and I placed the ring on her finger, but she wore it only for a moment, took it off again, handed it back to me, stood up, and said, "Take me home."

The final drive back to her parents' house was our longest and quietest. When I came to a stop, she opened her door without saying a word.

"Wait," I said while pretending to reach behind my seat, "I have something for you."

She didn't turn around and made it all the way inside the house, shutting the door behind her, without once looking back.

The next day I called her and asked if she'd have lunch with me and, surprisingly, she agreed. (I once again didn't take "NO!" for an answer.) She summoned her courage and drove to meet me.

"How could you lead me on and then dump me? Don't you care for me at all?" I asked. As if to stab her, I confessed I'd lied and had wanted to "screw" her from day one. My using "screw" instead of "sleep with" or "make love to" made her flinch.

"Thank you for being honest," she said with a satisfied smile.

The hardest part of the whole experience was returning the ring. It took me a week to locate the courage and I dragged Jenny along to play the role of almost-fiancée-who-isn't-ready-for-a-diamond. She played the part worthy of an Oscar and the saleswoman fell for it. Both women wept.

A few weeks later, Jenny came clean and told me Monica quit her job the day after our lunch, packed her belongings, and moved to Chicago to be with Michael. (I was the force that helped her overcome her inertia. She drove in Seattle. She moved to—and probably drove in—bigger and scarier Chicago.) I've since learned through the grapevine that they married and have two kids. I saw a family photo with him smiling in the foreground beside two boys, both holding tennis rackets. In soft focus, Monica receded into the background. Dressed for summer, she tugged on her shorts as if still trying to hide her legs from my eyes.

Looking at the photo opened my eyes. I barely recognized her. Love at first sight is perilous. During those three months I "knew" her, I often looked at her, but did I ever see her? After I wrote the words describing her a few chapters ago, I found a photo of Conny and Jenny's wedding party. Monica's hair wasn't flowing and blond. It was curly and brown.

~ *The King of Comedy* ~

FEELING DRAINED by my Monica episode, I paged through a magazine and came across an ad for a fancy Super 8 camera made by the French company Beaulieu. It had the ability to shoot slow motion. My Visa card jumped out of my wallet. I'd always enjoyed the ending to Michelangelo Antonioni's *Zabriskie Point* with a big, expensive cliff house and a bunch of refrigerators and wardrobes getting blown to bits, the slow-motion explosions protracted for minutes, debris floating in the air, early Pink Floyd music drifting from the theater speakers. Explosive filmmaking possibilities filled my emptiness.

By the time I held the camera a week later, my world-ending visions had dissipated, and I stared at a larger credit card balance than the one left by the diamond ring, but with no return possibility. I had few if any ideas for using my new toy. (Consider this a lesson not to make big impulse purchases after a breakup.)

I realized I didn't want to blow up Monica's world. I wanted to do something more creative. I chose to recreate the shower murder from *Psycho.* I didn't want black-and-white. I wanted vivid colors including splashes and splatters of bright red ketchup and I wanted everything to be in slow motion, to resemble my life.

Paul and I had a perfect tub and shower. I bought a Bugs Bunny shower curtain and curtain rings I could destroy for the occasion. I relocated the nearly lethal knife from my previous production and took stock of the required condiments in the fridge. The only thing missing was a victim. Monica had run away. *Jenny's a fine actress, but she'll never go for this*, I thought with a sigh. In short supply of people, I cast the always-up-for-anything Paul.

I drew a storyboard by renting a VHS and going through

the scene shot by shot. I paused the head on the tape so many times I ruined the scene for all future renters. We spent all afternoon collecting shots of water streaming out of the shower head, the knife stabbing at the air and clearly missing flesh, Paul's hand pulling at the shower curtain, the curtain ripping from the rings, and ketchup swirling around the drain. I popped the last cartridge out of the camera, drove to the drugstore, and mailed my footage away.

A week later I fetched the processed film, but my enthusiasm for the scene had evaporated. I couldn't stay mad at Monica—something about Aunt Gwen's advice. She'd once said, "You never know what they've been through." In Monica's case, except for my firsthand knowledge of her "being through" me, it rang especially true.

(Who am I kidding? I didn't find a photo of Monica and her young family "through the grapevine." I sat bored at work one day and Googled her. It's not that I wanted to somehow see—or at least look at—her again. She's long ago, in a city far, far away, but I do think about her. I want to ask her if she's *still* okay.)

I tossed the three reels of film from one hand to the other and wondered, *Is that it?* I took one of the reels out of its box, held the footage to the light, and reenacted a famous image of Jean-Luc Godard peering through a strip of celluloid. The images looked bright and colorful. I pulled my projector from its box, set up my screen (which Paul had given to me as a Christmas gift) and settled in to watch the rushes. I hadn't run any tests with the camera and, to get the movie shot in one afternoon, I'd mostly neglected using a tripod and instead balanced the camera in my hands. The slow-motion shots looked terrific the few times I *had* used a tripod. But all the handheld footage jittered as if the film had flown off the sprockets. My heart sank. I watched it a second time to be sure and tossed the film into a drawer to become parts never belonging to any movie. I dropped the camera back into its box and pushed it to the back of the top shelf in my closet. I ditched it.

A few months later, I sold the camera to a coworker for $300. At a net loss of $1800, I moved beyond Monica while Paul mostly regretted ruining the Bugs Bunny shower curtain in the process.

PAUL INVITED me to a Halloween party, and I racked my brain for days, conjuring the perfect costume. Inspiration flashed. I hit thrift stores and rummaged through clothing. I returned home again, a few hours later, amazed I'd only needed to visit two stores to buy everything.

The night of the party arrived, and I donned my costume. It consisted of a white dress shirt, gold polka-dotted blazer, red bow tie, red hankie in the pocket, and a fake mustache. My hair (what little hair I had) was dyed black, greased, and combed back. As I emerged from my bedroom, Paul, dressed as a pirate, took one look at me, and said, "Are you who I think you are?"

"Oh, I'm sure I am," I said.

"Yo ho, yo ho, I'm going to need me a whole bottle of rum," he said.

We hopped into his car and away we went.

At the party, my costume selection went well. Women said hi and flirted with curiosity. Enjoying the mystery of my identity, they asked me to dance from all directions. Guys eyed me with jealousy.

After dancing with each woman, I'd ask her, "Would you like to see a picture of my pride and joy?"

When she'd say yes, I'd whip out an index card with pictures of a bottle of Pride furniture wax beside a bottle of Joy dish soap I'd clipped from magazines.

She'd grimace. When another song started playing, she'd wander away to find someone else to dance with. After three dances, I found myself standing alone by the refreshments table, pouring a plastic cup of punch, and wishing it contained twice the alcohol. I glanced across the room and all three of my dance partners stood in a semi-circle talking and looking in my direction. When they noticed me watching, they looked away and laughed.

Driving home, Paul said, "Why didn't you tell me you were

going as Rupert Pupkin?"

If you have no idea who Rupert Pupkin is, you're in the majority. He's a character played by Robert De Niro in the movie *The King of Comedy*, a comedian who is so unfunny, hapless, and such a loser he kidnaps the host of *The Tonight Show*, played by Jerry Lewis, to demand five minutes on national television before being arrested. (He was worth less than fifteen minutes of fame.) He's an inspiration for Joaquin Phoenix's Joker. I doubt my interpretation came across any less creepy.

I've always suspected Paul phoned Jenny the same night.

"Hi Jenny. Uh…"

"Something wrong, Paul?"

"Well, yeah, kinda."

"Out with it."

"You gotta find Todd someone else to date. Please. He's killing me."

"Paul. I'm trying, but I'm fresh out of single ladies."

~officially fool-serious~

I SAT at my desk, eating my usual pb w/o j (my lengthy morning showers often forced me to abbreviate my lunch before dashing out the door) while studying an issue of the *Seattle Weekly*. The subject of my fascination: an ad for the Seattle International Film Festival. I gave it a shot but acted too late for buying tickets and few were available. The long lines also frustrated me. They left me sitting in lousy seats, often in the front row by the outer aisle.

The following year, I started early. They offered a full series pass; it sounded perfect, and as I recall it cost about $140. Feeling wealthy, I bought one.

I had the run of the place. For a screening of *My Life as a Dog*, a line wrapped around the Egyptian theater, but I bypassed it and headed straight for the short VIP line by the doors. A woman stood ahead of me. She came across as free-spirited. While I'd always wished I'd been old enough to attend Woodstock, she might have been one of the teens rolling around in the mud. She chatted with people near her in line. Frequently, her infectious laugh burst forth.

As I entered the theater, she turned toward me.

"Hi," she said, "I'm Annie. I don't think I've seen you here before. What's your name?"

"Todd. Nice to meet you."

The movie is a delightful Swedish coming-of-age dramedy about a twelve-year-old boy, Ingemar, who comes to terms with his mother's terminal illness. It's bittersweet all over the place.

Or that's all the movie meant to me back in 1987. I watched it again, for the second time, at age fifty-eight, and, as with *E.T.*, it felt as if I were watching myself. Ingemar spends his days playing—and chatting—with his dog, a mutt that reminds me of Princess and, while recalling the story of a boy who was electrocuted while swinging from a live wire, he decides that pretending to be Tarzan isn't the safest of activities.

Sent away to spend time with his uncle while his mother, who is dying from tuberculosis, rests and tries to recover, Ingemar falls into a new society of children. One child becomes the center of his experience, an attractive tomboy named Saga. She has convinced the other children she's a boy so she can play soccer, but she confides in Ingemar. Her breasts are budding, and she needs his help to conceal them. He tightens her bandage and assures her they don't show. She rewards him by giving him boxing lessons.

He returns home to visit his mother only to experience her final days and hours. Back onto the train he goes, back to live with his uncle. (Throughout the movie, Ingemar's father is "halfway around the world.")

Ingemar and Saga reunite. He's ready to resume where they left off and put his gloves back on, but she's changed. Her breasts have grown beyond the point of fooling anybody and she no longer wants Ingemar to help her conceal them. She shows them to him. She wants him to feel them. He flees.

Ingemar *is* curious about women's bodies. A dying man enlists him to read to him from the pages of a lingerie catalog and Ingemar's eyes gleam as he does so. He crashes through a skylight while glimpsing a neighbor woman's nude body as she poses for a sculptor. But Saga's up-close-and-willing flesh is too intimate. When Saga and another girl fight over him at a party, he reverts to barking as a dog.

I had my own experience with a tomboy as a twelve-year-old. I was playing soccer during lunch recess and a girl named Kathy kicked the ball on the opposing side. At one point, I tripped her (by accident) and her mouth filled with turf. She punched me in the gut. Boys laughed as I doubled over, but she didn't. She studied my reaction.

Weeks later, our class prepared for the annual May Day dance. Kathy passed me a note asking me to be her square dance partner. I crumpled it. I'd already arranged my partner for the dance, another girl-shy boy named Timothy. We drew an eight-foot-by-eight-foot square on the playground asphalt with chalk, put on boxing gloves, and spent the entire duration of the square dance's music sparring. It exhausted us and we dripped with sweat. By the end of the match, we had a cheering section of half the boys in the lower classes. Kathy spent the dance with a different partner.

By age fourteen, Kathy had grown into the prettiest girl in my class. I had a crush on her, but I wasn't alone. She had her hands full. Sometimes girls are like movies and movies are like girls—you first experience them when they're ready for you, but you still have maturing to do before you catch up to them. One of my favorite activities is revisiting movies every ten years or so (or in this case thirty-three years later) and seeing how our relationship has changed. (It seems I was wrong, many pages back. Pictures *aren't* always the same every time we see them.)

"You're officially fool-serious," Annie said as the credits rolled.

"I'm what?"

"That's how we refer to full series pass holders."

"Ah, full series, fool-serious. I like it," I said and we both laughed.

Walking out of the theater and into the night, we exchanged goodbyes.

"See you tomorrow," she said.

I attended a midnight screening of the movie *Street Trash*. I sprawled out across three seats with a blanket and a pillow. Yawning and knowing I had another foolish day of movies ahead of me in a mere nine hours, I left as soon as it ended and headed home to sleep, but Seattle freeways had plans too. I sat stuck till dawn on the 405 as a tank truck and two compact former-cars blocked the two lanes, all three in a ball of flames. I nodded off the entire next day.

Mid-festival, Annie and I took advantage of an extended break between movies. A war movie from Finland was screening and didn't interest either of us. (We didn't miss anything. The print they apologetically screened had shown up direct from Cannes, in Finnish with French subtitles.) While heading to the restaurant, I left Annie in the dust, walking briskly. I needed to pee and hated using the theater's tiny men's room with two exposed urinals and one stall with a curtain. Seeing ghouls crawl out of public toilets in *Street Trash* hadn't helped either.

"Wait up!" I heard her shout.

She chose a table. I headed straight to the men's room.

"Are you okay?" she asked as I rejoined her.

"Much better."

We had a nice chat.

"I've been into movies for a short time," I said. "It started while watching *8 ½* in college."

"Wonderful movie!"

"It sure is. It blew me away," I said. "Have you seen *Vagabond* by Agnès Varda?"

"I did."

"What did you think?"

"I enjoyed it. Her documentaries are even better. She did a terrific one about the Black Panthers."

"Oh. I'm fascinated by the Sixties. I'll have to check it out."

We both enjoyed talking with someone else who knew what the heck we were talking about.

"I make movies, too," I said.

"Oh. What kind?"

"Silly things with my friends getting drunk and stuff."

"I'd like to see them." (She would see one of them, years later. She said I was a fine director. I remember her compliment meaning the world to me.)

"That can be arranged," I said.

MY LIFE as a Dog won the Golden Space Needle Award for best picture, but I voted for *Wings of Desire*, a stunning movie about angels comforting troubled souls in Berlin. I always found the bits-of-paper voting system for the award suspicious. The same people always lurked by the ballot box.

Standing out in front of the Egyptian, Annie and I said our goodbyes.

"See you next year," I said with a smile.

"Definitely," she said, with less of a smile.

We walked in opposite directions to our cars.

Why "next year?" We had a lot in common. We should've gone to movies regularly. What might have happened if we'd parked our cars in the same direction?

The day after the festival ended, I experienced a worse case of the Mondays than ever. I sat at my desk at work ignoring a pile of test procedures I was being paid to edit. Instead, while I flipped through my dog-eared festival program, one of my eight or so bosses watched me for a while before walking over to my desk.

"Yeah. I think you should read the Bible instead of that thing, *mmm* 'kay?" he suggested.

It'd be a while before I realized the reason for his advice.

What made me think I could get away with such behavior? Had I been hypnotized?

~happiest place on earth~

ONCE UPON a time after I first found opera, I'd wandered into Tower Records and purchased enough opera CDs to cause the store clerk's mouth to form a huge "O" like a character out of a *Far Side* cartoon as I whipped out my Visa card. I was at it again, buying a towering stack of opera CDs, the entire Sir Georg Solti interpretation of *Der Ring des Nibelungen*, adding meaning to the store's towering name. Wagner's four opera cycle, lasting fifteen hours, includes gods, heroes, dragons, a castle in the sky, love triangles, magic swords, and Valkyries in its epic sweep. All I knew going in was one of its famous themes blares out of the helicopter-mounted speakers in *Apocalypse Now*, Bugs Bunny and Elmer Fudd spoofed it in *What's Opera Doc?*, and it's opera's equivalent of *The Lord of the Rings*. Seattle Opera famously stages it on a regular basis. I'd overhear talk about it between acts at the opera house.

"Lots of opera," the Tower clerk said. "I've never seen anyone spend so much at one time." He searched beneath the counter for a plastic bag large enough to hold my haul. It filled two.

I smiled as he handed back my credit card and drove straight home.

I had two weeks before the cycle commenced with the merely two-and-a-half-hour long *Das Rheingold*, the cycle's prologue. I had lots of mythology to figure out. I wanted to spend the performances focused on the music and I knew it would be my thing. It had a dwarf and a magic ring. I spent every evening and every waking hour during the intervening weekend flat on my back on my living room floor wearing headphones, popping CDs in and out of my player, and following along in the libretto books until they were dog-eared and frayed.

On opening night, I stood in line well before the doors opened. As the bolts released and the double doors swung inward, we filed into the opera house in orderly fashion, a well-behaved and solemn variation of a rock concert. As I found my seat and surveyed the place, I thought, *So many people, all strangers*. It attracted a nerdier than usual opera crowd. People dressed casually and sat alone. I suppose it's not easy to talk a date into such a commitment. I glanced at a few of the solo women and wondered if they might be potential ladies of my future, but they were all content to be alone and a few hid behind open books. The nearest held a copy of *Middlemarch*. I returned my attention to my program and the music ahead.

As those four evenings unfolded, I sat enraptured. I barely felt those fifteen hours. I'd never encountered the music of Wagner (except, and I didn't realize at the time, the wedding march from *Lohengrin*) before I'd unwrapped those CDs. It isn't light and airy like Mozart. It's serious and ebbs and surges and flows. I recognized it as a predecessor to Bernard Herrmann's score for Hitchcock's *Vertigo*—lushly, darkly romantic.

When the cycle concluded, it looped around for a second fifteen hours of devoted couples and assorted loners. Intoxicated after the performance of *Siegfried*, I'd checked with the box office for ticket availability and discovered decent single seats still available. I drove home with one for each opera. As I settled into *Das Rheingold* again, something happened. As I observed the other opera goers, once again holding nineteenth century novels to avoid unwanted conversation, I realized how they reminded me of…me.

I don't recall my specific thoughts until the intermission of *Die Walküre* (during which I slipped out into the night never to return, leaving my final two tickets unused), but it may as well have been about how my situation hadn't changed since high school grad night.

My high school—same as all prosperous ones in Southern California—participated in Grad Night at Disneyland. We ditched our gowns, said goodbye to our proud parents, and piled into buses headed for the Magic Kingdom. We had the run of the place all night long. I hit Space Mountain, twice. I floated through the Pirates of the Caribbean. I gazed across the water at Tom Sawyer's Island and wished I could explore it in the dark, but found the gates locked, no boats running. Instead, its shores had been converted into a stage for KC and the Sunshine Band. Listening to their set, I could no longer ignore one simple fact. I'd enjoyed all my favorite rides, several times because of the short lines—alone. With everything around me converted into a dance floor, I was miserable in the happiest place on Earth.

I took a break from opera. I'd head into the city and browse Elliott Bay Books, drawn toward Charles Bukowski's *Women* and a decidedly different Burroughs (William S.). *Naked Lunch*, "a frozen moment when everyone sees what is on the end of every fork," became my constant companion. (I never have made much sense out of that book.)

I read Burroughs's *The Ticket That Exploded* as well. He wrote of words as being like a virus. Try to close your mind to language and you'll fail. Words will fight against your resistance and force you to think, to talk. Words had been accumulating within me my whole life. They would break free during my quiet times when alone—or at least when I thought I was. (Some of my most embarrassing moments have been when caught talking to myself.) Something approached to set them free publicly—although I wasn't yet aware of its coming.

I made excuses for my loneliness by becoming obsessed with books lurking on the least frequented shelves of the city. I became God's lonely man. I'd drift into Jazz Alley and sit at the bar, order a beer and bourbon, and sulk, glancing over my shoulder each time the door opened to become Bukowski's alter ego Henry Chinaski as played by Mickey Rourke in the movie *Barfly*. I'd watch as women strayed in from the street, but none resembling Faye Dunaway ever sat beside me. I tried to ignore that I hated bars. What was I doing?

As with every public place in the city I'd ever visited, the bar included a *Seattle Weekly* stack. I set aside the pages of *Women* and flipped through an issue. An opera singer, Leontyne Price, who had been on my radar for a while, was scheduled to perform a recital at the opera house. I didn't need further encouragement. A few weeks later found me seated near the same seats as during my times with Wagner. Price even performed Wagner's "Mild und leise" from *Tristan und Isolde*. I wandered back out onto the rain-shiny Seattle streets once again—and forever since—an opera lover.

I sat in my apartment all night listening to Price sing Verdi's "La Vergine degli Angeli" from *La Forza del Destino* on repeat with wet eyes.

~"Sultans of Swing" days~

ONE PICTURE I discovered in Mom's boxes of slides is of her and me sitting on the couch. She's pressing an open magazine into my lap. It's hard to tell if she's reading to me or using the magazine to prevent me from escaping. Covering the entirety of my head is the inflated white air bag of a portable hair dryer, a home version of ones used in beauty salons. The glare in my eyes is a silent wish to murder Dad for snapping the picture. Otherwise, the photo is typical in our family albums: Mom and I seated comfortably, content.

I remember a moment between Mom and me (around the time Mom told me to "get out of here!"). It came when Cheryl and I top-secretly hatched the perfect plan. *We* pretended to be houseguests in her bedroom. *We* discovered if you pull a dresser drawer out halfway and apply a blanket and pillow it makes a wonderful pull-out bed. *We* set it up. Cheryl climbed in and stretched out and on cue the dresser fell over and the drawer slid closed, trapping her inside screaming. Mom arrived in a flash and righted the furniture, freeing its captive. (Most of my childhood memories omit physical disability. She was Super Mom.) Sitting on the floor *beneath* me, Mom smothered Cheryl in hugs and pointed, sending me to my bedroom. The official story became *I* invented that deathtrap.

Dad, on the other hand and when present, towered *over* me—and my most vivid such memory involves toenails. It came from his days in the Navy. Every week, he'd gesture with his hand for me to strip my feet, so he could examine my toes. If I failed inspection, he'd go to the bathroom and grab the scissors, those dreaded scissors. I'd wiggle and wince as he cut my nails to conform to his standards. Clippers are bad enough, but scissors are painful beyond belief, at least the way he wielded them. My nails would be bent upward allowing the scissor blades to pry their way underneath. Thanks to him, by age ten, I had reason to run away. I once spent an entire day hiding on the roof to avoid the toenail scissor ordeal. I sunburned. I kneeled and peed into the rain gutter. Ever since, my toenails have tended toward the long, gnarled, and hideous.

I can't remember Dad ever comforting me. Once, as I entered puberty, I managed to injure one of my testicles—somehow, zipper maybe? I went to him in tears. I feared I might never exist without pain ever again. Worst of all, the notion of explaining my symptoms to a doctor terrified me. What if a nurse observed? I could barely tell Dad what ailed me and only did so by pointing between my legs and shifting back and forth between left foot and right.

"Get used to it. You're going to be sensitive from now on down there," he said as he stepped out of his teeny tiny briefs and into the shower.

But am I being fair to him? It's interesting how overall impressions of a person affect the memories we keep. I struggle to remember positive images of Dad, but I know he wasn't all bad. I have this one vivid memory of us. It's a rare just-the-two-of-us moment and I remember it because it says how hard he could try to be what a dad should be—and how difficult I could make it for him to succeed.

When I was nine or ten, he took me to a UCSB college football game. It should've been a happy, father and son bonding afternoon out, but I messed it up. During halftime, business-suited men advertising something, probably insurance, engaged the crowd by throwing white plastic footballs into the stands.

"I want one, Dad! Get me one! Jump higher, Dad!"

He made superhuman efforts to try to snag one as they soared over his head. He risked injury jumping in a grandstand to appease my fleeting desire for a worthless toy. He didn't snag one. Hardly anyone ever returns home from such an event with a prize. And he would've had to have been twenty feet tall to have had a chance.

I didn't speak to him for the rest of day. Have I ever given him a chance to be heroic? Nothing about the experience of writing this memoir has caused me more melancholy moments than the way Dad has shrunk until nearly vanishing. I enjoyed writing my portrait of him way back in the third chapter. He looked ridiculous as he played with his microwave oven, tried to assemble a TV, and longed to be a disco-dancing fool. I can't help but laugh. I long to write something about him comparable to Mom growing as I ran toward her on our front porch. I'd love to at least make him into a fool again. In this next passage, let's see if I can at least restore him to his height of five six.

MOM HATED driving. (When she had to surrender her license due to old age, I detected relief behind her worried voice.) She couldn't move her feet spryly from the gas pedal to the brake pedal and back again. She had to be careful to give herself plenty of stopping distance. She managed driving a less powerful car, her old Chevy Nova station wagon, but near the end of their marriage Dad bought his beloved Oldsmobile Cutlass with a V8 engine. Mom sat behind the wheel one day, due to necessity, and proceeded to give herself a terrible fright. She pulled out into a busy intersection and pushed on the gas, no harder than usual, but too hard for the unfamiliar Cutlass. Before she knew what had happened, the car spun on a patch of oil in the intersection, narrowly avoiding collisions. Observers must've figured her one wild lady, doing donuts in traffic. When the car came to rest, she sat terrified until a passing police officer came to her rescue.

She never drove the Cutlass ever again and feared driving anything anywhere for months. She forever became the slowest, most cautious driver in all of Goleta.

Dad became my driving teacher once I clutched my learner's permit and he'd drive across town—and come face-to-face with his ex-wife—each day to take me out for lessons. I recall those as our Dire Straits, "Sultans of Swing" days. The song played on the radio every time we went out driving. It's the one thing about those lessons I fondly remember. We both loved that song.

He looked relieved when the day arrived for my driving test. He was about to be off the hook, shedding himself of one of his few remaining parental responsibilities. When he saw the car returning to the station a mere five minutes into my test and the examining officer crawling out shaking his head, Dad knew my education wasn't over. I had managed to almost hit a pedestrian in a crosswalk and attempted to make a left turn from the right-most lane of a one-way street. The examiner wasted no time guiding me along the shortest and safest route back to the station.

A week later, I managed to pass the test, but Dad's driver training trials continued. He'd bought me my VW Bug with a stick shift, an optional challenge foolishly placed along with all prior compulsory driver training boxes to be checked.

I wish I could say Dad had the patience of a saint, but the impatience of the Grim Reaper would be a better description. He reached his breaking point (or was it braking point?) when I came to a stop on a hill in traffic. His lessons hadn't covered slopes yet and every time I'd attempt to move forward, I'd roll backward a foot or two, slam on the brakes, and stall the engine. He yelled instructions at me about "the parking brake" and "you have to be quicker" and then he reached over, set the brake, pushed the stick into neutral, and ordered me out of the car. He maneuvered over into the driver's seat and told me to hurry up, go around, and "just sit" as drivers behind us honked. He shut off the radio so he could concentrate while "Sultans of Swing" played—cutting it off mid-lyric—and drove us out of the predicament straight back to Mom's condo.

He never took me out driving again. I taught myself to drive stick in a parking lot over the next week or two. One day, while taking my first solo drive to Aunt Gwen's house, "Sultans of Swing" came on the radio and, when the song continued from where it had been cut off, I felt free.

Two tidbits about Dad—one family legend and the other my personal myth because I rode alone with him in the car when he told the story—make me realize he was not the best driving teacher I could've had.

When he was fourteen and living in Oklahoma, his dad had purchased a brand spanking new 1949 Ford Tudor sedan. It came in black with a white steering wheel. It must've been the sexiest thing on four wheels to him as a teenager. The press dubbed it "the savior of Ford" because it revived the automaker after WWII. Dad begged his dad to let him drive it. He barely knew how to turn the ignition key and didn't hold a license. Oklahoma had become the forty-fifth state to require driver's licenses in 1937, but the state wouldn't seriously enforce it until well after the war years. Oklahoma didn't have a standardized driving test until 1949.

Grandpa Carl forbade his son to drive his car on the street, his "wholesome boy."

Of course, Dad rebelled, a bad boy on a mission.

Grandpa Carl rose every morning at 3:00 a.m. to meet his coffee klatch. He was early to bed. The first Saturday night that two-door beauty sat unguarded, Dad stole the keys and hit the road. Or—and this is the funny part—he hit the sidewalk. No telling what Grandpa Carl had meant by not driving the car "on the street," but Dad took it literally. A small car plus wide sidewalks equaled joyride. He cruised for several blocks and several minutes until a cop flashed his red lights at him.

Grandpa Carl often lectured me about what trees make the best switches. He swore by lemon trees and had a dandy in his front yard back in 1949. I doubt Dad sat on anything—car seat or otherwise—for weeks.

The other tale comes from Dad in his middle age. In his early fifties during the late 1980s, he drove along California coastal Highway 1 shortly after dusk with me in the passenger seat. He wore a mischievous grin. He spun a fanciful monologue. I felt like Alvy Singer in *Annie Hall* being driven down a dark highway by Annie's brother Duane.

"I have this dream, Todd. There's this underground club around these parts with members stretching all the way from LA to San Francisco. They call themselves the 'Black Riders.' They wait until well after dark during the wee hours of the morning… probably two o'clock…and hit the road in long caravans. Their cars are all black…paint, windows, everything…and their headlights are black light. In the country, they're invisible and boy those cars are powerful. They go 130 miles per hour, easily. They'll fly right past cops and dare them to do anything about it."

"Uh-huh," I said, tightening my seat belt.

"If you're ever driving down the freeway late at night and feel a *whoosh* almost pushing you off the road, that was them," he added and laughed.

I'm not sure if the "Black Riders" were a thing or a figment of his imagination. My Google searches come up empty. Maybe it was like Fight Club—something people did but were forbidden to talk about.

(I'll leave this one to my readers. After those three driving-related tales, what's my final grade in Father's Legacy Resuscitation 101?)

After I moved to Seattle, Dad and I rarely spoke. I kept thinking there must have been something else going on. The blunder of not giving him the right CDs for Christmas wasn't an adequate explanation. When I visited Dad for the last time in California, he and his second wife stayed outside repairing a fence by the garden while I chatted with Grandma. His behavior felt odd, but I didn't question it.

Us Fords, we don't say much. We fix fences.

The next—and last—time I saw Dad happened five years later. I lived in North Dakota. He had divorced, again, and both of his parents had died. He no longer had a fixed address and wandered about in a fifth-wheel camper. When he visited, he parked his rig twenty-five miles away in a campground and drove into town to see me—once. He and I sat in the living room, awkwardly.

"I hear you're good with databases," he said.

"I'm so-so. I use Access."

"How'd you like to go into business together? I find clients and you build databases for them."

"No. I don't think so. I do enough of that at work already and I don't enjoy it there."

He frowned. He left. It's a shame. Doing something together involving computers could have been the first harmonious time of our lives together.

I've seldom heard of him—never from him—since. I'm left to imagine him driving the old California highways from coast to valley and border to border, occasionally alighting like a monarch in Monterey, until he empties his gas tank for the last time.

(Addendum: I did contact him by email after Mom's death. He was residing in southern New Mexico. He wrote: "I lost a lot out of my life the last 20 years and I hate it but it's in the past now. Things happened that I couldn't handle and the only thing I could do was to disappear." I also learned that he'd given me more than a propensity to run away. We both have glaucoma—which gifts me with the possibility of becoming a blind movie buff.)

A FEW months after my time with Monica, I arrived home at the condo and became annoyed. Somebody had parked in my space. I thought for a moment about boxing the car in, my front bumper touching its rear bumper and leaving a note, but decided the inevitable confrontation wasn't worth it.

I approached the front door with my keys in hand and reached for the doorknob but noticed the door ajar. I looked for Paul's car. I didn't see it. I hoped I hadn't failed to secure the door when I left for work. I cautiously went inside, turned the corner toward the bedrooms, and Paul's girlfriend, Mary, stepped out of the bathroom. She smiled at me.

"How did you get in here?" I asked.

"Paul gave me a key," she said, taking it out of her purse and dangling it before me.

I glared at her.

"I…was just leaving," she said.

"I…think so," I said.

When Paul opened the front door, I blew up.

"What made you think you could give her a key without asking me?"

"We've been dating for months. I thought it would be okay."

"Well, it's not."

I went into my bedroom and slammed the door.

After fuming for a day, I rented an apartment. I bailed on Paul, leaving him stuck with full rent on the condo. It's a sign of the true friend he is that he still talks to me.

I'd had it out for Mary from day one, and she hit her low point for me when we all spent a few days on a rented houseboat, along with her young daughter Ellie and Dragan and his wife Liz. Ellie sat beside me crying.

"Where's my mom?"

I knew. How the heck could I not have known? Houseboats aren't big. Ellie, precocious and smart, also knew. Mary and Paul had been in the tiny bathroom for half an hour. I knocked.

"Um, guys, there's a little girl out here who needs you."

"A few more minutes," Paul said. I heard Mary laugh.

I don't know which caused me more angst: Paul getting some or someone taking Paul away from me.

Moving day into my apartment was a lonely and tiring affair. When you're not speaking with your best friend, *you* haul all the boxes. I bought furniture—a couch and a queen-size bed—to make the place feel homey. Jenny helped me pick out linens and chewed me out for having one pillow.

"Come on, Todd. You act like you never plan to share your bed."

I hung Nastassja Kinski with boa above my dresser. I positioned Aunt Gwen's painting of David Innes spearing an alligator, an animation cell from *What's Opera Doc?*, and a poster for *Full Metal Jacket* in the living room. I watched Bugs Bunny leap into Elmer Fudd's arms, remembered a shower curtain from once upon a time, and missed Paul terribly.

Shortly after settling into my apartment, I had friends over for housewarming: Conny and Jenny and one of Conny's brothers, John. John and I hit it off from the start. Both rudderless ships adrift, we competed to see whose hairline would travel across his head the fastest. And we shared movie fever. He fantasized as often as I did about "making it" in Hollywood. He took a year off and wrote a feature-length screenplay. A doer, he spoke of waking in the middle of the night, his head swimming with ideas plucked from his dreams. He'd scribble them before they'd evaporate, or he'd drift back to sleep, or both.

Weeks before, he'd sent me (or handed me? I can't remember) a copy of his finished script titled *Rabid Transit.* He wanted me to read it, tell him what I thought, and encourage him. I was one of the few people he knew who would appreciate his creation.

At the end of the evening with chip crumbs and empty beer bottles on the kitchen counter and everyone drifting toward my door, we said our goodbyes.

"Todd. I have a friend who wants to read my script. Can I borrow it back for a while?" John asked.

My heart sank. I thought about lying. I should have lied. Lies were invented for such situations. But I'm a terrible liar.

"Uhh, I'm sorry. While moving, I threw it away."

An icy breeze passed through my curtains and lowered the room temperature by twenty degrees. All sense of excitement and hit-it-off-from-the-start friendship drained away. Nothing else was said, by anyone. The door opened, people walked out, the door closed.

I sat on my couch. "FUCK!" I shouted at nobody.

I haven't heard from him since. I knew how hard it is to write something, anything, and I understood the passion and tears behind those 180 pages.

I felt the loneliest I'd ever felt.

~"say 'what' again. i dare you"~

INITECH MAGNIFIED my loneliness. Recently I came across an Internet meme that expressed my state of mind back in those days. It showed a male ballet dancer leaping into an office building elevator. It bore the words: "Me on Friday." (It resembled my state of mind at the end of every workday.)

One day, a glimmer of possibility arrived: an intern named Charity. She was about twenty, had shoulder-length black hair, and wore a chaste, home-sewn dress. Conservatively dreamy.

I passed her desk a dozen times before saying hi.

She said hi right back, but nothing else. She didn't look up.

I took a breath and again said, "Hi." I don't know what I hoped would happen, but no phone cord wrapped around her, she still didn't make eye contact, and no file cabinets went tumbling.

After an hour and three wanderings past her desk, she acknowledged my smiles with faint sighs. (I wish she'd said, "Stop. There are things about me you can't handle." I'd hopefully learned *that* lesson.)

"Would you like to have lunch?" I asked.

"Why do you want to have lunch with me?"

"To get to know you."

"Why?"

"Why not?"

"That's not an answer," she said and returned to her work.

The day ended. I went home and thought about her. She hadn't said yes, but she hadn't literally said no, either. I decided to try again.

The Last Temptation of Christ was coming soon. On a Monday, a week and four days (I was counting) before the movie's opening, I walked toward Charity's desk and something about the way she glanced at me looked inviting—or less uninviting. I came to a stop and gave it a go.

"Would you go with me to a movie?" I asked.

"Um…maybe," she said. "What movie?"

"*The Last Temptation of Christ.* I've been dying to see it."

Her brow furrowed.

"What?" I asked.

"It's a horrible movie!"

"What?"

"Jesus has sex with a prostitute!"

"What?!" (I'm surprised she didn't say, "Say 'what' again. I dare you.")

"It's nothing like that," I continued. I knew it involved Jesus fantasizing while on the cross about marrying Mary Magdalene and impregnating her. I broke a sweat.

"How do you know?" she asked.

"I have a copy of the screenplay. I've read it. It's not what you've heard. Would you read it?"

She still glared, but said okay to get rid of me.

I didn't think it mattered. The copy of the screenplay I'd received had lost one page from the third act. I figured it stuck in a copy machine along the way. I brought it to work the next morning.

"Here it is," I said, holding it out for her. "It's missing page ninety-seven, but you get the…"

"Get away from me!" she said, refusing to take the bound pages.

Irritated, I stomped back to my desk.

For the next couple of days, as I walked past her desk, I didn't say anything. I barely looked at her. She mouthed hi at one point and I ignored her.

On Friday, a coworker and mutual friend ambled toward me.

"What's going on between you and Charity?" he asked. "She's very upset."

"Nothing," I said.

"It must be something."

He had a Holy Bible forever positioned on the corner of his desk. My safe reply: "I'd rather not talk about it."

On the following Monday, my supervisor called me into his office.

"You're being transferred back to Kent," he said.

"When?" I asked.

"Today."

I didn't put two and two together at the time. The news pleased me. I'd have a shorter drive to work each day and I wouldn't have to walk past Charity's desk ever again.

I saw *The Last Temptation of Christ* at the Cinerama Theater, alone, on opening day. Dozens of protesters outside harassed the people standing in line. Every one of them had shoulder-length black hair and a home-sewn dress. As I walked past them on the way into the theater, I gave one an angry snarl.

"Get a life!" I said.

She slapped me in the face. My eye was still watering as I took my seat.

Christian critics of the movie had it all wrong. Jesus does leave the cross, marries (twice), and sleeps with his wives, but it's a fantasy sequence brought about by chemicals in his brain as death draws near. The sequence is a variation on *The Wizard of Oz*. A gusty wind blows him from the cross, he wanders into a lush setting with colors more vivid than any we've previously experienced in the movie, and he lives his life as if he'd never been the Messiah. (Okay, it's also a variation on *It's a Wonderful Life*.) A wind whisks Jesus away from Golgotha and into the countryside same as a tornado carries Dorothy away from Kansas into the Land of Oz. And just as Dorothy realizes her mistake, clicks her heels, and finds herself in her bed again on the farm, Jesus notices his stigmata and crawls away from Judas back to the cross. His declaration of "It is accomplished!" should have delighted Christians everywhere.

~Christmas Eve night, 1977~

AFTER CHARITY, I readied to take a long break from women, work, and life to become a bum, write screenplays, sell everything, and make a real movie, but my mind seldom stays on one thing for long before losing focus. One day I'm buying books about politics and it's all I talk about. The next, I'm bored by politics and instead read about Charles Darwin.

Soon, a coworker from my new huge and monotonous Initech office building, Michelle, caught my eye. Or, for a change, I caught hers. An engineer as well, she was smart, wore glasses, and had her own shy, quiet streak. She might've been Amy Farrah Fowler to my Sheldon Cooper.

Michelle asked me out to lunch the day we met. We were late returning to the office. After work, we relaxed in the community hot tub at her apartment complex. She'd loaned me a pair of swim trunks her brother bought while visiting. We had a few beers and started making out. She hopped into my lap. She smelled wonderful. Her lips felt moist and sticky. She jumped off my lap, climbed out of the hot tub, and dove into the cold swimming pool. I thought about following as if it was her playful way of making the moment last, building anticipation, but I read her expression and a chill as frigid as the pool water washed over me. Something changed. A switch flipped.

We went back to her apartment and dried off and dressed, separately. We sat on her couch.

"What happened?" I asked.

She didn't answer. Instead, she took my hand and sucked on my fingers, one after another, somewhere between seductively and absentmindedly, and she sobbed. I didn't know what to do or say.

A short time later, she walked me out to my car, and I rolled down the window as I readied to turn the ignition key. She leaned against the door and said, "I lied. Those swim trunks aren't my brother's. They're my old boyfriend's and seeing and feeling you in them reminded me of him."

Neither of us said anything else. I drove away. And my drive home in the steady Seattle rain, albeit shorter, reminded me of my final drive home after breaking up with Monica. I'd lost another girlfriend to an ex-boyfriend. Why was I forever with women who would leave me for an old but not forgotten flame? Was I what they needed to prove what they'd had was special? Oddly, I felt relieved. I'd wasted three months on Monica. I'd cut my losses to a few hours with Michelle. I was getting the hang of this dating thing.

I broke the seal on a bottle of Jack Daniel's and sat in my living room in the dark. I wondered what would happen if I drank the entire bottle at once. I cursed Mom and Dad for setting such a horrible example.

CHERYL AND I were crazy kids when it came to Christmas mornings. We'd be out of bed and camped in our pajamas, each with a blanket, under the tree at 4:00 a.m., waiting for our inconsiderate parents to hurry and join us, a mound of presents waiting. Sure, I admit we were spoiled, but we were also compensating for something. We filled emptiness with train sets, western boots and saddles, and shiny bicycles.

On Christmas Eve night, 1977, it happened. I awoke during the middle of the night, long before 4:00 a.m., with a strange sense of unease. Something wasn't right, an unfamiliar draft, a faint rustling, a whisper. I walked down the hall toward my parents' room. The door was closed with a sliver of light beneath. I heard Mom crying. I opened the door and peeked inside. I peered through a dark passage with a pool of light at the end. In the light, I saw three separate visions that my mind failed at the time to assemble into a coherent story: (1) Dad kneeling beside the bed, his voice low, but scolding, his foot tapping as he held a waste basket, (2) Mom in the bed, moaning, and (3) a spilled bottle of white capsules on the nightstand.

I stood in the bedroom doorway watching, barely comprehending. When Dad saw me, he snapped his fingers and pointed me back to my bedroom. He followed me and closed my door. I stayed awake the rest of the night. I heard strange, muffled sounds coming from beyond my bedroom door, coughing sounds, walking around sounds, and water running and toilet flushing sounds. Did I also hear a strange man's voice? After a while, I buried my head under my pillow and faced the wall.

I blocked out the significance of what I saw on Mom's nightstand. I wasn't ready to process it. I didn't have any experience with *suicide*, the most foreign of words. When I watched the movie *Ordinary People*—and observed Mom's reactions to its two suicide attempts—one successful, one not—the meaning of those spilled pills choked me. Everything might've been even darker if Dad hadn't come home that night. To give me distance from a different troubling episode, I've renamed two characters in this memoir Conny and Bucky, after the tragic brothers in *Ordinary People*.

On a day like most others, I went to visit Conny and Jenny, but when I arrived, something felt amiss. Jenny answered the door crying. I heard the door to the master bedroom close. I assumed I'd interrupted a fight.

"What's the matter?" I asked.

"It's Bucky. He was in a motorcycle accident. He didn't survive."

I sat on the couch. I had few words for such a moment—or any other moment. I wondered if I should hold her and wondered if I should go check on Conny.

Jenny slowly, cautiously, sat beside me: "There's more. Bucky died with his motorcycle, but it wasn't an accident. He was beside it in the bathroom of his apartment."

Bucky was one of two people I've known to commit suicide. The other, a school buddy named Randy, went away to college, seemingly happy, returned home for Christmas, drove to the top of San Marcos Pass near Santa Barbara, and jumped.

Bucky's pushing his motorcycle into his bathroom, closing the door, stuffing towels in the cracks, and starting the engine will forever haunt me. In Randy's and Mom's case, I wonder how deep the pain must be to carry you over the threshold on what should be the most joyous day of the year. Suicide is the ultimate way of expressing oneself without resorting to words.

The next morning, Dad sat Cheryl and me in the dining room and told us he was leaving us. After he finished, he looked at the floor and left the room.

During the drive to Oxnard for our Christmas gathering, Mom pleaded, "Please, don't anybody say anything to my dad and mom and Gwen. My dad doesn't need to know yet." Her face glowed sickly pale.

It shouldn't have been happening to us. This happened to people in galaxies far, far away. I sat in the back seat and stared out the window at the ocean. Palm trees whizzed by while an offshore oil drilling platform on the distant horizon remained stationary. The illusion fascinated me. It's called the parallax effect. Early astronomers used it to calculate the distance to the nearest stars. (See? My mind darts all over the place.)

Tarzan, what would you *do?* I thought.

Todd, Edgar never wrote me into this *book*, he replied.

We arrived at their house, a long, rambling affair with ample space for horses on its one-acre lot, and settled in for breakfast. We opened presents. We lounged about. Aunt Gwen watched Cheryl ride her horse Katie. We ate dinner. Mom and Gramma Dirty spent a lot of time alone doing the dishes. Grampa Fred and I watched a show with Donnie and Marie Osmond on television while eating warm apple pie with melting vanilla ice cream. He put his arm around me. As we drove away, Grampa Fred was putting his jacket on and heading out to tuck the horses into bed for the night.

The drive home was quiet as well. All day long, nothing had been said about the divorce—no tears, only smiles. I relaxed. If we kept pretending, maybe the divorce really would go away. When we opened the front door, we heard the phone ringing. Dad picked it up, listened, and hung up. He turned to Mom and said, "That was Gwen. Fred had a heart attack. He's dead."

As Mom crumpled to the floor, Dad matter-of-factly told us kids to go to bed while they drove back to Oxnard to help Gramma Dirty and Aunt Gwen cope with the situation. Well into the early morning, they returned. Mom headed to the bedroom. Dad spent the rest of the night in the living room.

I've often wondered what happened during their car ride, the two of them driving an hour each way, divorcing, exhausted. Grampa Fred had died and the thought going through my mind was he had known, and it had broken his heart.

In the morning, Dad gathered all he needed and moved into an already rented apartment across town.

AFTER MY strange hot tub and couch experiences with Michelle, I sat in the dark, listening to the rain coming in sideways against my sliding glass door, and rather enjoying the gloom, until I turned on the light to go find a CD—anything besides *Jazz Samba*—and there it was, staring me in the eyes from the middle of the coffee table: a copy of the *Seattle Weekly*.

~ mellow, professional swm ~

FOR YEARS, I'd been skimming the *Weekly*. It had decent movie reviews, although *The Stranger* had my favorites. I'd ignore the personal ads. That night, though, I studied everything posted by single females. As I slept, mystery women wandered through my dreams. A few of those ads were by women wanting men for quick flings, one clearly wanted a replacement daddy for her kids, and one authored by a ballroom dancer wanted a man for "pinochle and more." The words "pinochle" and "more" waltzed in my head. I considered writing a screenplay titled "Pinochle and More." One ad—the grand prize winner—rose to the top of my fantasies. She described herself as "21, petite, red-haired, and a fan of The Butthole Surfers."

I had no idea what that last bit meant (more foreign language), but it filled me with curiosity. My high school had lots of surfers. I wished I'd known a few. (Too bad Google hadn't been invented yet. As I was editing this page while also reading Melissa Maerz's fantastic book *Alright, Alright, Alright: The Oral History of Richard Linklater's Dazed and Confused*, I learned a new tidbit about The Butthole Surfers. One of their drummers, Teresa Taylor, played the role of "Madonna Pap Smear Pusher" in Linklater's *Slacker*, a movie that impacted me profoundly in 1990, as you'll soon discover.) I composed a reply. It went, vaguely:

> *Dear Red-Headed Girl,*
> *I'd love to meet you. I love petite 21-year-olds. Um, what I really mean to say is I'd love to spend some time with you. You sound like a LOT of fun!!*
>
> *Sincerely, Ready for Anything*

I folded the letter, slid it into an envelope (mail moved like a snail in those days), addressed it to her assigned mailbox number at the *Seattle Weekly*, and away it went. Not surprisingly, I never heard from her and I could feel the blood warming my cheeks when, months later, something caught my eye while wandering the aisles of Silver Platters (a store chain for compact discs from back in the days when CDs were the thing). I've since become an avid fan. After listening to everything, I've decided *Hairway to Steven* is the band's masterpiece.

Shortly thereafter, while out about town, I located a fresh issue of the *Seattle Weekly* and for once didn't glance at the movie reviews. I headed straight to the back pages and read everything: women seeking men, men seeking women, women seeking women, and men seeking men. I became a student of all angles. IF I can figure this thing out, I might meet someone. Or ELSE, well, one can only watch *Dawn of the Dead* so many times.

Nothing jumped out at me and captured my imagination the way the red-headed girl had, but I kept reading. It struck me how often women write better than men. I also noticed no matter how hard men tried to sound as if they were sincerely looking for a loving and lasting relationship filled with back rubs and moonlit walks, all their ads resembled:

```
SWM seeks lots of women for casual one-night
stands, followed by a few seconds of cuddling,
um, scratch that last part.
```

I'm a better writer than these fools. I need to be honest (but not too honest) and playful and creative and I'll have women climbing all over me, I coached myself. So, I wrote—and had my boss's administrative assistant type—my own ad:

```
MELLOW, professional SWM, 26, 5'6", NONSMKR,
```

```
light drinker, no drugs, LOVES MUSIC from
Aerosmith to Miles Davis to Verdi, EMBRACES,
the Comedy Underground, hugs, Calvin and
Hobbes, nestling, The Far Side, cuddling,
ANIMALS of all kinds, snuggling, highly
original FILMS, slow dancing, and STAYING IN
SHAPE with racquetball, nautilus, swimming,
hiking, skiing (only the snow variety so far),
and eventually, with the right teacher, roller
skating around Green Lake. I play classical
guitar (okay, just learning) and consider KIDS
as more than okay. If you are intrigued by this
description and are an emotionally available
woman, 22-28 or so, who shares some of the
above, please drop me a note. I would love to
get acquainted and if things click…
```

Trembling, I slipped it into a mailbox. A week and a half later, I received a large manila envelope with *Seattle Weekly* in the return address. It felt a bit heavy. A few possibilities slid around inside. I climbed the stairs back to my apartment, poured Jack Daniel's over the rocks, tore open the envelope, and emptied three letters onto my coffee table. The envelopes arrived in different sizes and colors. The handwriting ranged from shaky printing to flowing calligraphy and each had its own unique aroma. One envelope smelled of pizza, one of perfume, and one of, well, something hard to place, as if trying not to be too conspicuous. I tore into the pizza.

Dear Mellow,

You sound fun. You sound odd, but not bad odd, just okay odd. I'm odd too. I'd love to cook dinner for you some time soon. I only know how to cook one thing, but I won't say what. I like surprises and hope you do too.

I should tell you something about me. I'm a blonde. I'm HWP [height weight proportionate]. I don't smoke much. I drink only when I'm sad. I'm 37. I've been married before. Long story…

Her letter went on for another page and a half. I remember feeling fearful as I read it. (I'm recreating two of these letters to the best of my memory because they've long since been discarded. I wish I'd held onto them. I have had a long history of tossing possessions when I no longer felt I needed them.) I refolded the letter, stuffed it back into the envelope, and pushed it to the far edge of the coffee table. I picked up the next letter, took a whiff of the perfume, and opened it.

Dear Huggy Guy,

I've never done anything like this before. I don't know what I'm doing. I need somebody to hold me all night long. Will you? You sound cuddly…

What have I done? I thought. I put the letter back into its envelope and placed it on the already-read side of the coffee table, a bit closer than the pizza. I took a sip of my drink and reached for the third envelope. Its being the final one, my last chance, worried me. *Have I mastered this dating thing so well my relationships last no time at all?*

I opened the envelope after curiously noting it had a return address. You weren't supposed to do that. I pulled out the letter, and something else fell out and fluttered to the floor. I turned it over, one of those tiny black-and-white photos you snap in a photo booth, a picture of a cute, twenty-something woman. I opened the letter, my heart rate increasing.

Dear Calvin and Hobbes Fan,

My name is Trissa. I am a single, non-smoking, 24-year-old. I love Calvin and Hobbes and Bloom County, and kids are definitely more than O.K. with me.

I work as a live-out nanny for a family with four kids. My BS degree is in education and I have an AA degree in computer science. I need a few more credits to acquire a teaching certification in Washington State.

As you can guess, I got the picture at one of those little picture booths. It was rather embarrassing, and I know you didn't ask for a picture, but I thought it would help. My hair is brown, and my eyes are green and the rest of me is a 5'6", shapely 145 lbs.

I'm sensitive, caring, patient, intelligent, honest, and in 1976 I won the title of "funniest girl in the eighth grade." I'm shy, but very warm after I know someone. I'm not into singles bars but love to slow dance. I don't meet many adults at work, so I decided to try answering personal ads.

I would appreciate a gentleman who is sensitive, caring, intelligent, patient, humorous, and willing to do anything spontaneously funny.

My interests are reading, laughing, travel, animals, nature, exploring, volleyball, softball, swimming, and I do know how to roller skate.

If you are interested, give me a call: (206) ___-____

Sincerely,
Trissa

I read it again. She had green eyes. In 1976, she had been the funniest girl in the eighth grade. I glanced again at the photo. She had shoulder-length, dark hair, and dark lips I imagined to be red. She reminded me of someone from my distant past from a sultry evening in Oklahoma. Was she—? I then had a nervous realization. I'd soon be dialing the number she had written at the bottom of her letter.

I hadn't thought beyond the moment when I'd written my ad and dropped it in a mailbox. I hadn't believed I would entertain any responses, but here I was holding a letter, complete with phone number and a photo, from a young woman I didn't know existed a few minutes before and who became all I could think about. I knew I had to call her. I wanted to see her step out of that black-and-white photo like Dorothy Gale and into my world of living color. Or was it me stepping out of my Kansas and into her Oz? Seattle *is* nicknamed the Emerald City after all.

I sipped my drink, noticed the ice had melted, poured it into the kitchen sink drain, and dialed her number. The phone rang. *Oh my God, what am I going to say?* I tried and failed to clear my throat. As I had with Enid, I thought, *I'll let it ring five times and hang up.* It rang once, twice, and a woman's voice said, "Hello."

A surprising thing happened. I said, "May I speak to Trissa?" and my throat relaxed. I felt calm from a combination of her voice and the letter and photo on the counter before me. I talked without my usual fits of nervousness.

"This is her," she said.

"I got your letter from the *Weekly* today. I read it several times and I'd like to meet you. My name is Todd."

"I'm sorry," she said, "which ad was yours? I replied to three."

I knew photo booth pictures came in strips of three.

"I'm the guy who wants to learn to roller skate around Green Lake."

"Oh, I remember. It was sweet and different from the others."

"Different as in good?"

"Yes! You're a terrific writer."

"I loved your letter too and want to meet you." I said.

"My sister has been freaked out about my doing this personal ad thing and she told me to only meet with guys in public places."

"I understand. This whole thing *is* kind of weird."

She laughed. "I remember you described yourself as being mellow. Most city guys I've met haven't exactly been mellow."

"Well, I'm not really a city guy. I grew up in a fairly small town in Southern California. It was by the beach, so that kind of made me mellow."

"Oh, that explains why you like to swim. I bet you were a

surfer."

"No. That's one of the things I didn't do, although recently I wished I had."

"Why do you say that?"

"Just something I read. Anyway, the water at the beach is way too cold. I just like watching and listening to the waves."

"I keep forgetting. The ocean is cold in California. It was so warm in Florida."

"You've been to Florida?"

"Um, yeah. Let's just say it was one of my mistakes. I like that you're from a smaller town. I'm not a big city girl either. I grew up in North Dakota."

"I bet the water's pretty cold there, too."

"It wasn't too bad in the summer. My family would swim in the river far enough to reach a sand bar. Most swimming pools are indoors though."

We chatted for a while and I did finally pop the big question of the moment.

"Are you free to meet somewhere tonight?" I asked.

"Tonight won't work. I already have a date."

My heart sank, but she threw it a life preserver.

"How about tomorrow night? Between you and me, I don't think tonight is going to go well," she said. (She later confessed our talk threw off her schedule. Her date had to wait as she applied her makeup.)

"A Saturday night is perfect. Where?" I asked.

"Do you know Capitol Hill?"

"Are you kidding? It's my second home," I said, my excitement growing. (Capitol Hill is Seattle movie central.)

"Let's meet in the Dick's parking lot. We'll walk from there, unless you want burgers."

"Seven o'clock? Boondocks? It's a block or so from Dick's."

"We have a date," she said.

"Goodni— Um, I have a picture of you, but how will you recognize me?" I asked.

"What do you look like?"

"I'll be wearing a tan jacket. I'm about five six. Oh wait. I guess you already know that."

"Tan?"

"Yeah, it's warm. It's corduroy with a lambskin collar."

"Corduroy? Lambskin? I see. I'll be in a yellow Chevette. We'll figure it out. See you later, Scott."

"You mean Todd?"

"Yes. See you tomorrow, Todd."

She hung up.

I've always been fascinated by how our lives would be changed if seemingly insignificant events had played out differently. If the *Seattle Weekly* hadn't been sitting on my coffee table on my gloomiest evening, the rest of this tale would be different. It would be as if the Scarecrow and Dorothy had chosen a different road—or as if Dorothy had never landed in Oz at all, leaving the Scarecrow stuck on his post forever.

I also lucked out. I ran my ad twice. The first time, it was typed up by someone at the *Weekly* who accidentally omitted my age. I got zero responses. I first thought, *Oh well. I tried.* Then I got brave, phoned them, probably trembling, and complained. They ran it again for free with the added "26."

~...and i blew it~

I SPENT Friday night fretting while Trissa and a guy (Scott?) were surely enjoying their date. I ran through our phone conversation endlessly. Had I said anything stupid? By bedtime, I'd convinced myself I was less than a day away from being stood up. I spent Saturday pacing about my apartment, glancing at her photo, rereading her letter.

I arrived on Capitol Hill forty-five minutes early. I had plenty of time to find legal street parking. I didn't want to spend another evening of tea and coconut cookies with elderly oddball strangers. It still took four attempts to squeeze my car into a space while two handsome young men with well-groomed beards took a break from necking on their front porch to enjoy the show. I parked four feet from the curb, three, two. They applauded when I opened the passenger door, glanced out, and decided a foot and a half away and a bit crooked was close enough. I thought of Alvy Singer's line in *Annie Hall* after Annie's slapdash parking job: "We can walk to the curb from here."

I had to trudge six blocks to Dick's. To kill time and catch my breath after the hike, I settled into a bookstore within view of the drive-in, flipped through books by the front window, and watched for the arrival of a yellow Chevette. It also occurred to me my vantage point would allow me to evaluate my semi-blind date before committing. I've always felt safe in bookstores.

I'd opened a copy of *Fantastic Mr. Fox*, reminiscing, when something yellow blurred through my peripheral vision. My date was pulling into the Dick's parking lot. I glanced at my watch—precisely 7:00. After being ridiculously early, I was soon to be officially late. I had no time for evaluation. I stashed the book back on the shelf and sprinted out the door.

I watched her seated in her car as I left the bookstore, walked away from her to the end of the block, waited for the light to change, crossed using the crosswalk, and approached her. I saw her face brighten in the side mirror as she took her first look at me. I placed a hand on the roof of her car and leaned toward her open window, as James Dean as I could muster.

"You must be Trissa."

"I am. And you must be Todd."

As she hopped out of the car, I saw all of her. She looked cuter in color. We strolled toward Boondocks. Her curves modeled blue jeans and a sweater, and she knew how to make the most of minimal makeup. She wore casual well. She was ready for a date, while I was a dork in a tan corduroy jacket I'd owned ever since I had been a teenage dork. (I don't totally consider "dork" to be a negative term. I always hear it coming out of Quentin Tarantino's mouth as he describes Jules and Vincent in *Pulp Fiction*—two of the coolest dudes around. I was—and still am—uncool-dorky though.)

Excited to be in her presence, I walked too fast and had to slow and let her catch up. Then I overcompensated and lagged. I took advantage of the fleeting moment to check out her curves from a better angle, but she turned and caught me in the act as we neared the restaurant door and I braced for a Monica-esque tongue-lashing. Instead, she flashed me a quick smile.

I'd called ahead, and we were seated immediately.

"Guys I usually go out with are so spontaneous," she said.

I hoped she was complimenting me and not them. (It was a good thing I didn't have her letter in hand to refer to.)

"You can have anything you want," I said.

"I may have soup and salad," she said.

"I'm going to have steak. You can too."

"Okay."

She flipped two pages deeper into the menu. "I'll have the fillet then. Um, how do you order it if you want it pink inside?"

"Medium rare."

The waiter came and went.

"I work at Initech," I said, obviously trying to impress.

She nodded and smiled encouragingly. "Initech's a great place to work," she said. "My mom, my Auntie Ruth, and my dad all worked there. My mom and Ruth moved here to work during the war. My mom was a Rosie the Riveter while Ruth worked for thirty-five years as a supervisor. I'm not sure what my dad did there other than meet my mom. He spent the war in the Army."

She gave me my first positive thoughts about Initech in years. The date felt a natural continuation of our conversation from the day before. She was a breath of fresh air and easy and fun to talk to. I recall my bragging about being an engineer as being the only time I felt the need to impress. I relaxed.

"So, you're a nanny?" I asked.

"Yep, I love it."

"Must feel wonderful," I said with a sigh.

"It's never boring. Every day is different."

"Tell me more."

"The two boys are kinda clingy. There're a bunch of steps from the street to their house and they always want me to carry them both at the same time. They're like twenty-six pounds each. They cry if I don't. And if I picked up groceries, I make two trips and they cry anyway, waiting for me inside the door."

"Ah, sounds like they like you a lot."

"I love them, too. The cutest thing is around nap time. If the TV is on and we can hear the theme song from *The Young and the Restless*, they both start yawning and saying, 'Nigh' nigh' babies.' Their older sister, Megan, told me their first nanny was a soap opera fan and would always put them to bed before airtime. They'd fall asleep listening to the music drifting up from the living room."

"That's funny."

"The middle child, Molly, could only fall asleep for her naps if I sat beside her bed."

She thought for a moment, her expression contented.

"I guess most of my nanny work is pretty boring," she finally said.

"No, it sounds sweet."

"Well, an interesting thing happened in my nanny life when I worked for this rich couple in Aspen. I knew someone who fell while skiing and was helped to his feet by Jack Nicholson."

"How did you end up in Aspen?" I asked.

"Well, it wasn't one of my brightest moves," she said. "The people I worked for turned out to be kind of horrible."

"I wish *I* could see Jack Nicholson," I said. *Dad, not so much*, I thought.

"Yeah, it was cool."

"So, what's your favorite book?" I asked.

"I love *The Lord of the Rings*. I've read it three times since I was thirteen."

"Me too. I had a class in high school where all we did was read Tolkien. It was hippie-ish down in California."

"Sounds like it, but the best kind of hippie-ish."

The waiter arrived with a bottle of wine. I'd ordered a chardonnay because she said red gave her a headache. We watched as he poured two glasses.

"You wrote that you love movies," she said as our glasses clinked. "Have you seen any movie stars in California?"

"Well, it's not like people think. It's not like there're stars on every street corner. I did see Jeff Bridges once."

"Oh, I'd love to see him sometime."

(She *would* see him, on a street corner in Seattle a year later, during the filming of *The Fabulous Baker Boys*.)

"It was when my high school band was extras in a movie. There he was. Twenty feet away."

"What movie?"

"It was this great one called *Cutter's Way*."

"I don't think I've heard of it."

"Um, few people have." I sighed. "Do you ever go to the opera?"

"No, why?"

"I've been going for years. Ever since I saw *The Magic Flute*, I've been in love. I'll take you if you'd like."

"My sister will be happy to hear that. She's an opera singer."

"Oh wow, I'd love to meet her."

"I'm sure you will."

After leaving the restaurant, we walked and talked all over Capitol Hill after dark. I was calm, sensing the date must be going well. We bumped elbows. She led the conversation, and I didn't notice the topics had long since strayed well outside of my usual dating non-chitchat. She was deciding if our pilot would become a series. I'm glad I was blissfully unaware of this. Nerves might have kicked in and who knows what I might've said.

"Are you a churchgoer?" she asked.

"I went to a Presbyterian church when I was growing up, but haven't found a church here in Seattle yet," I said.

"My family has gone to this beautiful Presbyterian Church in Mandan, North Dakota my whole life," she said. "I'd love to show you the stained glass windows." She paused. "So, you say you like kids?"

"I do. I come from a small family, just two kids. I'd like to have about the same number of kids, or maybe three, someday."

"My family is large. I have four older brothers and sisters. I was the 'oops' child, but they had me and here I am. Five may be too many for me. I think three kids would be perfect," she said. "I hope at least one of my kids has red hair."

"Why's that?" I was more than a bit curious.

"My family is full of redheads. Irish blood. My mom, my older sister and brothers."

"Same with my family. My mom and sister both have red hair."

After my "red hair" remarks—and it was a subtle thing—she started walking a bit closer to me. Our elbows bumped more frequently.

"And you're a pet lover?" she asked.

"I am. I had a dog named Princess when I was a kid. I miss her."

"I can't wait for you to meet my cat," she said. "His name is Al Lee Kat."

We eventually stood at Dick's in a nearly empty parking lot. I prepared to say good night and start walking when she said, "Get in. I'll drive you to your car." As I hopped in, she said, "I'd love to help you pick out a new jacket."

In the span of a couple of hours, she'd asked me if I wanted children, invited me to her place to meet her cat, allowed me—a blind date—to hop into the car with her, and spoken of wanting to help me shop for clothes. I shouldn't have been worried about a second date, but I was, and I blew it. While opening the car door, I said good night, hopped out, smiled, and waved as she drove away, her taillights becoming tiny red dots.

~unlucky in love~

I IMAGINE you're rolling our date through your head and thinking: *Why didn't you kiss her? You were such a doofus.*

I was already falling in love with Trissa…but…I'd kissed Monica at the end of our first date—too soon or wrong for her. I'd kissed Michelle in the hot tub on our "date"—and reminded her of her ex-boyfriend. With Trissa, I tried to take it slow, when I should have followed my urges. I was an understandable doofus.

The day after our date, I went to a grocery store and picked out a card. On the front were the words, "Just dropping a line to keep in touch…" The card's interior said,"…with someone who is liked so much! Have A Good Day!" Inside, I continued the sentiments:

Trissa,

Your letter caught my eye. Your voice soothed me. Your presence finished me off. Thanks for a great evening! It was my ideal first date and I didn't want it to end.

Talk to you soon,
Todd

Once again, as I had with Shelly and Tarzan had with Jane, I'd sent a note. I wonder if Grandpa Carl would've kept this one.

I mailed the card on a Sunday. By Tuesday night, I couldn't wait any longer. I dialed her number, and a man answered.

I nearly hung up. "May I speak to Trissa, please?"

"Hold on," he said, and as an afterthought, "Who's calling?"

"Todd."

I could hear a discussion in the background along with her voice.

"Hi, Todd?"

"Yes. Hi. Did you get my card?"

"I did, this afternoon. It was sweet. No guy ever sent me a card after a date before."

"I meant every word. I'd love to see you again."

"I'd like to see you again, too, but there's a problem. My date from the other night called me again and we're going out this Saturday."

"Oh," I said, trying and failing not to sound crushed.

"Can you call me on Sunday? We'll talk then."

"Okay." What else could I have said?

I trudged to my couch and collapsed. Before me, the coffee table remained a shrine to my *Seattle Weekly* adventure, Trissa's letter still unfolded with her photo sitting beside it. I looked at her picture and felt a wave of utter hopelessness. I no longer knew how to read her smiling face in the photo. I thought our date had gone well. I'd finally figured out how to act on a date; I'd been myself and I'd been beyond myself. And yet, I was, again, losing a lovely woman to another guy. I awoke that morning thinking I'd finally earned a passing grade. After that phone call, I considered dropping out.

I refolded her letter with the photo tucked inside, stuffed it back into the envelope, and slid it to the upper right corner of my coffee table. She didn't have my phone number. She couldn't call me. I could forget all about her and save her the trouble of telling me no. She did know where I lived. I'd foolishly written my return address on the card's envelope. I figured I could toss any letter she might send me. Or hoped she'd write me a bunch of letters, begging me to be her boyfriend.

I glanced over at the two letters by other women, beckoning from the opposite corner of the coffee table. I reached for the nearest and took a whiff. I imagined a forever mystery woman spraying a puff of perfume on the envelope after sealing it. I pulled out the letter and reread it. Her words—"I just know I need somebody to hold me all night long"—still sounded desperate. They made me think of the character whom Jimmy Stewart calls Miss Lonely Hearts in the movie *Rear Window.* I pictured her spending her evenings making candlelit dinners for herself and an imaginary guest, dressing up, and pantomiming romance before bursting into tears. I folded her letter and placed it back in its envelope for the last time.

I opened the pizza-smelling letter and reread it.

> *...I've been married before. Long story but one I thought I'd share.*
>
> *I met him while in college. He was such a romantic. He read me poetry on our first date. We had our first kiss atop Snoqualmie Falls. We'd take endless drives up and down the coast in his VW Bus. We'd make love everywhere. One time, we did it on the beach during the middle of the day. Another time, we did it in the changing room once I'd approved his tux for our wedding.*
>
> *Our wedding day was beautiful, and our honeymoon was playful. I was imagining us growing old, but, sadly, he was growing in a different way. He was becoming quieter and distracted. He started spending a lot of time at his job and he hated that job. One day, he came home looking pale. I moved to hold and kiss him, but he stopped me. He told me he was in love with someone else.*
>
> *I hate it, but yes, I smoke, I drink, I'm 37...*

I remember rather cruelly thinking, *what a cliché.* But stereotypes exist because they capture a truth. They're the average of everyone's experience. They're something everyone understands.

I saw Aunt Gwen in those words. I saw Cheryl. And I saw Mom. The women in my family have all been unlucky in love. Aunt Gwen experienced a serious but sadly temporary relationship. It's a foggy story, having happened before I came along. All I know is how she reacted to being rejected. She fell apart.

She became a smoker, a habit I hated. (Okay, she smoked all along. She's rebellious in teenage photos.) I once seized every pack of Marlboro Lights she had scattered about her house, dumped them into her bathroom sink, and turned on the faucet full blast. I cackled so gleefully over the destruction I failed to hear her enter the bathroom behind me until it was too late. I remember her face lit ominously from below, though such a lighting setup was impossible.

Aunt Gwen became hooked on romance novels, devouring a dozen a week and stuffing the shelves of three bookcases in her bedroom to overflowing. Barbara Cartland and Janet Dailey linger in my mind. I once spent an entire afternoon rearranging the books by publisher. When I finished, she had a stunning three and a half shelves of perfectly aligned red roosters. Her scowl inspired new impossible shadow effects and me to master the arts of alphabetization and looking up copyright dates.

Cheryl, through her writing, has learned one hard and fast rule: All romance novels must end happily ever after, part of the allure for Aunt Gwen, I'm sure. I also figure she enjoyed the brawny, long-haired guys on the book covers as much as I enjoyed staring at Dejah Thoris on the covers of *my* precious paperbacks.

The saddest turn Aunt Gwen's life took: her declining health. She ate junk food and her weight climbed. She'd breathe heavily merely walking about and the smoking gave her a hacking cough. She also spent hours out in the blazing Southern California sun caring for her horses, burned daily, and worried us as one scabby, bleeding growth after another sprouted on her face, neck, and upper chest. I know she never saw a doctor. Every time I asked her, she told me she had an appointment to have the "warts removed"—"next week."

One day, Mom called.

"Todd. Gwen had a heart attack. She's dead," she said, her voice shaking.

Aunt Gwen died trying to unlock her apartment door while

juggling bags of groceries. To add insult, her purse, watch, and jewelry had been stolen from her dead body. While in town for her funeral, I helped clean her apartment. It wasn't in a state of expecting company.

Whoever Aunt Gwen had been in love with, I hope he at least broke up with her gently, but I've always imagined he either stopped calling her or she'd caught him with another woman.

I suspect Cheryl's romance writing is a reaction to her own heartbreak. She was in a relationship with a young man named Tim. (I met him a few times but never really talked to him, and all I remember is he once gave me a copy of William Gibson's *Neuromancer* for Christmas and told me one day actors would be obsolete. "Digital 'actors' are easier to work with," he asserted. With a movie rumored to be in development starring James Dean, a digital Lazarus, Tim may have been a prophet.)

Cheryl phoned long-distance during her times with Tim.

"It bothers me you moved away and left me stuck with everything," she said nervously. (I'm paraphrasing. She caught me off guard, and I don't remember her exact words.)

She continued. I listened. She sounded outside her comfort zone. She hates confrontation as much as I do. I didn't say anything. There wasn't anything I could say. I agreed with her. The call was part of a therapy thing she and Tim tried—or I imagine Tim dragged her into. I suspect he listened to every word she said to me.

I don't know how their relationship ended, but it was one-sided (by him) and devastating (to her). I went through boxes of Mom's photos, and chronologically arranged pictures of Cheryl as a happy girl, Cheryl and a pensive Tim on various occasions ranging from Thanksgiving at Mom's to Cheryl's graduation from veterinary school, and just Cheryl again, looking glum. (And, yes, I'm aware the emotions I read in those photos are affected by hindsight.)

I'm sure both Aunt Gwen and Cheryl, if I'd told them about Monica, would've offered me the same advice as Mom did. "Take your time. Don't get hurt. And, please, don't do the hurting," she'd told me. She didn't want history to repeat as part of *my* life's love story.

Dad had cheated on Mom. The night Mom swallowed the sleeping pills, she'd learned he'd slept with Vera. And thinking back throughout my childhood, I don't remember happy times between my parents. I don't remember them ever kissing. I don't remember them ever sitting and relaxing and talking. The only photo I have from their dating thing is Mom standing on a New Mexico roadside mischievously hurtling a snowball at Dad.

While going through Mom's belongings, I came across a scrapbook. It's filled with ephemera from Mom's college graduation trip to Hawaii, Mom and Dad's courtship, and their wedding. I paged through it feeling grateful I'd found such a prized possession. I came upon a two-page spread celebrating their paper anniversary. Their cards to each other are glued on facing pages. Mom wrote, "I will love you another 80 years for sure. Love, Bev." Dad simply wrote, "Tom." I turned the page to find nothing. The rest of the pages…empty. With those two cards, their scrapbook story ends.

I duck away from those memories to recall happier times with Mom. As a child, I'd spend days with her at the beach. She'd buy me a new plastic pail and shovel every time because I was notorious for losing or breaking things (made of plastic or otherwise). She'd set me free to make sandcastles—random, collapsing mounds of wet sand—as she stood and watched, and *where* she stood was always the same. As if she had a looking glass and foresaw my future scuba diving near-drowning, she feared my going near the surf. One photo after another in my shoeboxes tells the same tale. I built my "castles" while sitting in the dry sand. She stood in the wet sand between me and the infinite ocean.

When I moved to Seattle, I thought I'd made it. An engineer, I attended my five-year high school reunion (the only one I've attended) as a celebrity, a person in my class already out in the world making serious money. My head bursting, I tried to buy a car. I'd driven my hand-me-down red Toyota Corolla to Washington, but Mom had promised it to Cheryl as soon as I could replace it and I soon had my heart set on a sexy blue

Honda CRX. I visited a showroom, saw one, and made the salesman's job ridiculously easy.

"Let's start the paperwork," I said.

"Okay, son," he said, looking me over.

After the easy stuff (my name, my address), he asked, "How long have you worked for Initech?"

"Several months."

He dropped his pen. *Clunk.*

"I'm afraid I'm going to need a co-signer. Can you come back with your dad?"

"Um."

I left the dealership dejected and phoned Mom. She agreed to put her credit on the line and the next day, after various documents had been faxed back and forth, I drove away in my bachelormobile. I felt as cool as Bruce Wayne cruising Gotham City in his Batmobile. (Which version of that sleek car you picture in your head is up to you. I still prefer the one with Adam West behind the wheel and flames shooting out the back.) Going through Mom's file cabinet while waiting for her funeral, I found copies of all those loan forms still saved in an envelope labeled "Things for Todd."

If a place of business treated Mom nicely, she'd be a devoted patron for life. For years, she drove all the way across town to use the same gas station because they'd still hop out of the convenience store and pump her gas, check her oil, and clean her windshield as if her arrival had turned the clock back to the sixties. She continued to travel across town to the same hairdresser her whole life because, she'd say, "Betty is so kind."

My favorite of these memories is of her being the See's Candy Lady. Every candy holiday—Valentine's Day and Christmas and Halloween (and not-so-candy ones such as Thanksgiving or I-felt-like-it-in-August)—she'd send out those fancy white boxes. It wasn't the candy. She was as prone to leaving a few half-nibbled chunks of funny, fruity-tasting confections as anyone. It all stemmed from her experience of walking into one of their stores. They had been friendly. The last time I visited her, she made me go to the store in La Cumbre

Plaza, her favorite location, to purchase special shamrock candies.

"And make sure to ask them for a sample. They keep them behind the counter and don't advertise them. They're for special customers," she told me with a wink.

I've relied on a scrapbook, boxes of photos, and the convenience of saying, "Before I came along" (words echoing those once used by Dad) as I write about three of the most important women in my life. I wish I'd talked more with them. And I mean talked about real stuff. IF I had, this whole memoir wouldn't have been necessary. This dating thing would've been as natural as breathing—or, maybe, I'm now showing a whole new form of naïveté.

Mom always had a way of guiding me when I needed it. Her words "don't get hurt" and "don't do the hurting" rang in my ears. I gently placed the woman's letter with its "long story" on the coffee table. It didn't feel right to put it back into the envelope, at least not right away. I glanced back at Trissa's letter, picked it up, opened it, and stared at her phone number. I felt certain she would say no on Sunday, but I had to at least give her the chance to say maybe or maybe yes.

I stared at one huge IF.

~our bed~

ON SUNDAY, I dialed Trissa's number, and she answered after one ring.

"Hi Trissa, I'm um—"

She cut me off. "Hi, Todd, I was waiting for you to call and hoping you'd call. Are you free tonight? Would you like to go out?"

"More than anything," I said, feeling wobbly. "Where would you like to meet?"

"Todd, you have my address."

"Oh yeah."

"Why didn't you kiss me? I wanted you to." She didn't wait for me to answer. She said, "I have to run. Pick me up at seven," and hung up.

I hadn't been told to "get lost" and/or "have a nice life." Was this how dating was supposed to feel?

At 7:00 sharp, I sat in my car and studied her place, a tiny downtown single-story without a driveway or a usable garage, leaving you no choice except to park in the street every time you return home. I lucked out. A space awaited my arrival right out front, three cars in length—doable even for me.

A woman who resembled Trissa answered the door and let me in. A young man, a bit older than me and with a beard, sat on the couch reading *Architectural Digest.* A Balinese cat, still a kitten, sat on the back of the couch rubbing against his head.

Trissa emerged from a bedroom. She looked more ready for a date than the first time, leaving me speechless. Without a word from me, she took my hand and led me out the door. I glanced over my shoulder at the man and woman. They studied me closely.

She hopped into my car and I climbed in beside her. I said,

"Those two people. Your sister and her boyfriend?"

"Yeah. Marilyn and Rob."

"They looked worried."

"They're still not crazy about this personal ad thing. They even followed us for a while during our date. They swear it was an accident."

"Oh, that's understandable. I could be a crazy person."

"Yeah, maybe you are." She smiled.

"I haven't made any plans. What would you like to do?" I asked. (I *had* memorized her letter by this point, especially the "spontaneously funny" part.)

"Let's drive over by the waterfront and sit and talk."

At the end of a short drive, a parking space overlooking Puget Sound waited for us.

I shut off the engine and she said, "Why are you still wearing that jacket?"

"I was cold." I started to take it off and as soon as I popped open the last snap, she joined me inside it, and we kissed.

Far more than a memory of Grampa Fred's freshly plucked peach flooded my senses.

"Are you still cold?" she asked a while later.

I shook my head.

Once we finished properly and belatedly ending our first date, I suggested we see a movie and grab something to eat. I chose *Crossing Delancey*, a romantic comedy with Amy Irving, who works in a bookstore, and Peter Riegert, who plays a pickle vendor. It was a fun and pleasant flick and one of my rare wise date movie choices. We dined at Pagliacci's Pizza, a mutual favorite. She'd been there with her sister; I'd been there many times, alone, after a movie. I'd baffle the staff by ordering an anchovy and artichoke heart pizza "to go" and sitting at a table to eat half of it before heading out the door. I let Trissa pick the pizza: goat cheese and spinach.

We spent our third date at her house. Rob had settled in after a long day at the office. Getting kicked out wasn't scheduled for the evening and he learned about the plans as I watched. He wanted and deserved the lasagna bubbling in the oven for his dinner. Trissa and Marilyn stepped into a bedroom. Marilyn and Rob went away. Finally, Trissa and Rob talked. When they returned, he put on his jacket.

During the negotiations, I sat on the couch and scratched Al Lee Kat behind the ears. I figured befriending her cat to be a worthwhile plan. Al Lee Kat settled into my lap with a contented purr as Rob and Marilyn made their exit and Trissa joined us on the couch.

"Sorry," she said.

"Alone at last," I said, glancing at my lap, "almost."

Pets are aware of what's going on. Al Lee Kat knew he was being left out. He kept nudging his way in between us, becoming a wedge forcing us apart. I'd stroke his fur and gently, patiently, place him on the floor where he would stay long enough for my attention to return to his mommy. He would then wedge his way in again with increasing determination. And when he did this, he moved so slowly that his motion was barely detectable until too late. Our cat-and-man game wasn't going unnoticed either. How I behaved around her persistent feline protector was a test. The slightest hint of roughness or impatience would have been the same as being rude to a waitress.

For most guys, what happened next—once she placed Al Lee Kat on the floor and gave him a push—would've been the moment they'd been waiting for. But damn, I was so dense (or distracted by a cat) I failed to seize the moment. Trissa was wearing a buttoned sweater with a few top buttons open and underneath it a bra fastened in the front. As we changed positions and she hovered above me, her bra came unfastened, her cleavage on the verge of making an entrance.

"Uh-oh," she said, "my bra came undone."

When I'd had a stripper in my lap, I couldn't help but dive in. I'd had Monica before me and had taken advantage of whatever-had-happened to go for it. Perhaps Monica's reaction was guiding my actions with Trissa.

"Let me help you," I said as I assisted her back into her bra. I even asked her to help me refasten it.

We continued making out, but she seemed distracted. (Was

she disappointed I acted the way I did when her bra came unfastened? I turned and asked her after writing that sentence. She said, "Todd, you and your imagination.") When Rob and Marilyn returned home, we called it a night and kissed as I walked out the door.

I've always been fond of the scene in *Fast Times at Ridgemont High* where Stacy nudges Mark Ratner into her bedroom and attempts to seduce him. She throws herself at him and he splits. She fails in the short term but lands him in the long run. Mark and I need patient women. Otherwise, we're doomed.

(I wasn't as hapless as Mark Ratner. While preparing for his big date with Stacy, he's advised, above all else, to put on side one of *Led Zeppelin IV*. Cut to the young couple heading to the restaurant with "Kashmir" playing. I knew my Zep. I wouldn't have screwed that up. Once a date took her seat in my car, the first sounds she would have heard would've been "Black Dog." Yeah, Mark deserved to have his sister's tape deck stolen. He wasn't worthy.)

The day after "the bra incident," Trissa drove to my place "to see my apartment." When I opened the door to let her in, she stood there looking at me with a peculiar smile.

"What?" I asked.

"Are you a virgin?" she asked in reply.

I nodded shyly. She came inside and closed the door.

I FOLLOWED through on my promise to take Trissa to the opera. Gluck's *Orphée et Eurydice* appeared next on the schedule and I managed to convert my one ticket into two somewhat less optimal but nevertheless enjoyable seats. It's a tragic mythological story about two lovers. Eurydice is bitten on the foot by a poisonous snake and dies. Orphée descends into the underworld to find her and bring her back. He's made a deal with Cupid. If he can lead her all the way back to the land of the living without looking back to gaze upon her, she can remain with him. It's mythology. I'm sure you know how it turns out.

I've been in love with the story and the music ever since. I wrote a screenplay titled *Love in a Time of Zombies* where a woman named Samantha is bitten by a zombie and, after she turns, her boyfriend, Finn, allows her to bite him so he can be with her for eternity. I didn't fully understand the myth, though, when I wrote that script. I thought it was about a young man who is so in love he chooses to follow a woman into death. It wasn't until recently while watching *Portrait of a Lady on Fire* that I discovered a more powerful interpretation. In that movie, one lover explains to the other that Orphée made a choice by glancing back at Eurydice. He chose to remember her rather than to be with her.

"He doesn't make the lover's choice, but the poet's," she says.

I often think the poet's choice is the best choice, as heartbreaking as it may seem at the time. At least once, though, one must make the lover's choice, keep walking, and not turn around. I wonder how Orphée's memoir might have continued if he hadn't looked back.

After the performance, I took Trissa to the same quaint dessert place around the corner I'd once visited with Diane and her daughter Kelsey. We shared chocolate cheesecake and enjoyed cups of herbal tea and relaxing conversation about opera and my hopes to hear Marilyn sing someday. Dating became fun and I no longer had to worry about kisses goodnight.

For Christmas, Trissa traveled home to North Dakota and I remained in Kent. Absence makes the heart grow fonder. All week I wished I'd stowed away in her Chevette. I spent New Year's Eve night reading *Fahrenheit 451*. I was on fire when she arrived back the next day. Unfortunately, so was Trissa. She spent the next few days in bed with the flu.

It took a few months and several sleepover nights taking her away from Al Lee Kat before we decided to move the two of them under my roof. Fortunately, my apartment complex's management accepted pets. On her move-in day, she relaxed, her head hanging over the edge of *our* bed, which included *her* pillow, as she stroked Al Lee Kat's fur and watched me upside down as I rearranged my books to make room for hers. She loves Star Trek and Anne McCaffrey. I gave her a kiss.

I showed Trissa my collection of homemade movies. She watched my friends play poker, get smashed, and slither about on the floor and she thought it "creative." She watched my one acting performance as a spurned, evil hitchhiker and she couldn't believe it was me. I was a better actor than I thought. ("No, Todd. You weren't," she just told me with a laugh from across the living room.) She cringed when I told her about Dragan falling on the butcher knife.

"When it looks like he's starting to fall right before you cut away, was that when it happened?" she asked.

"Yeah."

"I can't believe you left it in."

"I cut out the part where you can barely see him fall on the knife. Anyway, something came of it. I don't drink and direct anymore."

"Do you still direct?"

"Not lately, but I'm starting to get ideas."

"Should I be scared?"

"Probably."

She soon realized dating me meant seeing lots of artsy movies. I frequented the old Neptune Theater, a revival house in the part of Seattle bordering the University of Washington—the "U District." The entire interior of the theater had been painted blue. Patrons felt submerged under the sea. The place smelled moldy and felt soggy. I ignored the dampness because they'd show evening-long programs full of cinema deliciousness. I saw *Polyester* with Scratch 'n Sniff cards and discovered a new way to laugh at Dad. I caught *Nashville* huge and sprawling across the wide screen and daydreamed about 1975.

There I "treated" Trissa to a David Lynch triple bill. It kicked off with *The Grandmother*, a short about an abused boy who spends the story cowering, making strange whining sounds, wetting his bed, and growing an elderly woman out of a pile of dirt in his bedroom. He needs a grandmother to have someone to love him. I looked over at Trissa and she was as pale as the boy.

Next up: *Eraserhead*. It tells the tale of a twisted young man who impregnates a woman and suffers from the worst case of fear of parenthood ever imagined by a warped human mind. The resulting baby, a deformed, reptilian creature, spends the movie crying in misery. The mother can't take it any longer and runs away, leaving the father and baby alone to run a vaporizer and barely survive, horribly. He eventually tries to put the baby out of its misery only to discover it's not too keen on the idea.

I'd read about *Eraserhead* beforehand and knew Trissa, a nanny, loved and cared for babies as if it was her purpose on Earth. What went through her mind as she watched it? Was she wondering what man enjoys such a movie?

I sensed her suffering. "Would you like to leave?" I asked.

"No, we'll stay. You've wanted to see these movies."

The evening concluded with *Blue Velvet*, and by the time Isabella Rossellini had stripped naked and held a knife to Kyle MacLachlan's throat, Trissa was trying to cover her eyes *and* plug her ears.

She's not a fan of Laura Dern, but she would've empathized with her character, Lula, from Lynch's next movie, *Wild at Heart.* To escape from the theater, Trissa wanted to tap her shoes together and be somewhere, anywhere else. Glinda might've descended from the heavens in a pink bubble to whisk her away. (To this day, every time *Eraserhead* is raised in conversation, she declares, "I hate that movie!")

My grade in Dating 101, with the help of Trissa's tutoring, worked its way toward passing, but my general elective in Date Night Movie Picking still threatened to expel me.

She avoided movies for a while. *Her* favorite is *Raising Arizona.* It has cute babies EVERYWHERE! That's her idea of a date movie. We also found a shared love for *Planes, Trains and Automobiles* and *Parenthood.* She'll see anything if Steve Martin is in there somewhere. His "This is all I need!" routine from *The Jerk* is such a favorite for both of us we find ourselves slipping it into conversation as often as possible.

When the time felt right, I coaxed her out to see what I knew would be a funny, light comedy. *The Naked Gun.*

Here we go again. Another movie and it has "naked" in the title this time. I wonder if Isabella Rossellini is in this one too, she surely thought.

Soon after *The Naked Gun* began, she felt safe, and she witnessed something else as well. Every bit of inspired slapstick comedy made me laugh harder until I did something I'd never done before but didn't find at all embarrassing. I leaned against her with my head on her shoulder, happy tears streaming.

She loved it. She loved watching me love it. She told me months later it was the first occasion she realized I wasn't too serious for her, the first moment she considered marrying me. With Valentine's Day around the corner, the same wheels turned in both our minds.

~"you are my density"~

MY GIRLFRIEND knew what she wanted, and she wanted me—something refreshing in my dating life. Trissa made our relationship unambiguous. She hinted at marriage, twice.

We were infrequent mall-goers, but on one of our rare visits she stopped me in front of a jewelry store and pointed at a diamond ring in the window.

"I love it. It's called a marquee," she said.

Diamond shopping was a piece of cake for my second go-around. No need for Jenny to tag along whistling "Shine on You Crazy Diamond."

During an evening in our bedroom, I folded a basket of clothes while she sat on our bed going through a box of heart-shaped candies. She joined me in the walk-in closet.

"I found you a perfect candy," she said.

I took it and started to pop it into my mouth, but she stopped me and a glance from her eyes told me to read the words on the candy.

MARRY ME

She watched my reaction and returned to her candy sorting, preparing Valentine bags for the kids she cared for as a nanny. What was my outward reaction when I read the words on the candy? I don't know. I hope it didn't disappoint her. My inward reaction was relief. I became certain my plan for our post-Valentine's Day dinner would end well. We both avoid crowds. Actual Valentine's Day is a night to stay in.

I wanted to propose at an upscale restaurant, and she'd

expressed interest in trying the Space Needle's sky-high revolving Emerald Suite.

"I'd love to go there for a special occasion," she once said, with a nudge.

Thinking well ahead, two days after her pillow joined mine on our bed, I'd phoned for a reservation and, as parking spaces by the waterfront were forever available to us, they had an open table for our big night.

We dressed for the evening and while she finished her makeup, I retrieved the ring from deep in my sock drawer, took it out of its box, took one last quick look while holding it to the light, and dropped it into my pocket.

Upon arriving at the restaurant, we had a short wait before being seated. We sat close, her hand on my leg, and I feared she would feel the ring through my slacks. At one point, she surely *had* felt it as her hand rubbed against the ring and rolled it over and over through the fabric. She may have been way ahead of me. (Okay, I'm sure she was.)

Our Valentine's Day, Space Needle, where would he have the ring? In his "pocketses"?

During dinner, I must have appeared preoccupied. She asked, "Is everything okay? You seem quiet."

"No. Yes, everything's okay," I said.

I knew I should hurry up. I reached into my pocket and fished for the ring. For a moment, my fingers didn't find it and my heart rate quickened. I slid my fingers a bit deeper and felt it. With the ring in my hand, I smiled and said, "I love you."

"I love you, too," she said.

I reached my hands toward her atop the table. She reached to take hold of them. I turned my left hand over showing her the ring sparkling by candlelight. I knew I better say it, say it simply, and say it quickly.

"Trissa, will you marry me?"

She held out her left hand. I passed the ring to my right hand and slid it onto her ring finger. She was in tears, happy tears. I leaned across the table and kissed her. I'm sure the food tasted delicious, but neither of us remembers it.

In bed, she asked me, "Did I say yes?" I noted the tears still on her cheeks and nodded.

She became the exclamation mark at the end of a line of girls and women for me, after my babysitter's daughter, then Kendi, Shelly, Anny, Sue, Janie (not Jayne), LeeAnne, Enid, Monica, Charity, and Michelle. Thanks to words being set free, I knew more about Trissa and she more about me before we officially met than all my shared "intimacies" with all the prior girls/women combined. With her help, I did figure out this dating thing. Maybe not an A+ yet, but hopefully I'm not being too easy of a grader by giving myself an A-.

I'm charmed by the honesty of Trissa's initial letter to me. The honesty of my ad was iffy. For one thing, I've never ever had any desire to roller-skate, around Green Lake or anywhere else. And all those references to hugs? I've never been a huggy guy—although I've gotten more into it as I've aged. I was as awkward about embraces as Sheldon Cooper, patting Penny lightly on her back. While I surely thought, at the time, that such self-description would be attractive to women, deceit wasn't my motivation. I was wishing my own adult love life would improve upon what I'd witnessed between Mom and Dad.

The relaxed openness of Trissa's and my relationship has continued to this day. We never fight. We sit every Saturday morning with cats in our laps, drinking coffee, and talking about paleontology, politics, and parenting. We take Amtrak trips to mountain lodges to do nothing but sit before roaring fires reading books. We both adore the train.

And, yeah, I love that she loves Steve Martin.

I GAVE her a ring three months after we met. We married six months later, on August 19, 1989, in a church on Bainbridge Island. The wedding party and our few dozen guests enjoyed the full Seattle experience by riding the Winslow Ferry for the occasion. The twins from her nanny life, Andy and Jay, shared the ring-bearing duties with a mixture of cute smiles and I-don't-want-to-do-this grimaces. We both sobbed as Marilyn sang the aria "O Mio Babbino Caro" right before our exchange of vows. I'd never heard her sing a full aria. Crying never felt so good.

Mom and Trissa's mom collapsed at the end of the wedding day. A photo exists of them sitting on a pew, shoes off, kicking their feet, two playful girls. Once again, few pictures survive to prove Dad's presence.

I'd chosen Mike Kim to be my best man and he sounded relieved when I told him I didn't want a bachelor party. It would've been too out-of-character for him. This disappointed Paul. He wanted another go at hiring a stripper.

At the reception, Mike acted nervous, but, when his time arrived to propose a toast, he proceeded undeterred.

"Ch-cha-chance is always p-p-powerful. Let your hook be always ca-ca-cast. In the pool where you least expect it, there will be a f-fish."

He'd been taken by my tale of casting a personal ad out into the sea of women and searched for a perfect quote by his favorite poet, Ovid. We'd taken a Classics class. *Metamorphoses* had been required and he read it three times.

"And what a lovely f-f-f-fish you caught, D-D-Dodd."

Mike and I also shared a sad moment before he left town. I remarked I'd feel honored to be his best man when the day came. He became contemplative. He ordered the one drink I'd ever seen him have. Putting him on his plane back to California was the last time I've seen or heard from him. His phone: disconnected.

Paul was my second groomsman, so Mary and her daughter Ellie were guests. Our wedding was one of the final scenes of Paul and Mary's relationship. He broke up with her soon after.

As I settled into married life, Paul and I drifted apart. I assumed he re-donned his pirate costume and had greater success without Rupert Pupkin tagging along. Then, as if no time had passed at all, he told me he'd met someone. On a lark, he'd participated in a bachelor auction and he'd fallen for his highest bidder: Tina. We had them over for dinner and she charmed us as well.

They married about eight years after we did. Not long ago, I asked them for details about the auction, thinking it far in the past and forgotten, and learned they too had memorabilia. They emailed me his page from the auction catalog: Bachelor #14. His personal description read:

> *Paul is an easy-going, casual, sociable, but energetic person. He feels as comfortable in a crowd as he does with one person or alone. Paul is the curious type, always wanting to explore new things and new places.*
>
> *He enjoys bicycling, backpacking, swimming, skiing, and generally going out to 'play.' He also likes to share the finer things in life like good food, wine, and music with a good friend.*
>
> *His ideal date: "Come downtown to the water with me and we'll cruise Elliot Bay on the Spirit of Puget Sound. After a delicious dinner with a wonderful view of the city, we will return to land and complete the evening at the club of your choice."*

Had he been inspired by my personal ad? I love how we each found our soul mate by writing about ourselves and courageously publishing it to the world.

Tina told me her winning bid was $175, half of it picked up by a friend (and "official half-owner" of Paul) as a birthday gift.

"When Paul came to our table to meet me, we had a 'moment.' I also got cold feet and tried to let him off the hook," she said, "but he soldiered on."

If Mike had still been around, he would've said, "Every lover is a soldier," once again quoting Ovid.

Paul says, "I'm socially clueless and meeting women was always difficult for me, so when a friend asked if I would like to be auctioned off to a room full of women, I said 'sure.' My biggest fear was nobody would bid on me."

They split the one contractual date into two, so they could take in both the Spirit of Puget Sound and the Giggles comedy club. During the date at Giggles, Paul says Tina phoned her mom and told her, "Don't worry. He's not an axe murderer."

Arriving for the cruise, Paul asked if she'd like to be

dropped off by the pier or if she'd walk with him from wherever he found a parking space.

"I'll walk with you," she said. "Look. I'm wearing my basketball shoes!" she added while pointing at her high heels.

Paul says, "I thought, *Hey! She's funny. I LIKE her!*"

WHEN TRISSA and I settled into the Sorrento Hotel for our wedding night and hopped onto the queen-size bed, she asked me to remove my ring. I looked at her fearfully.

"Don't worry. I want you to put it right back on again and leave it on forever," she said.

I took it off. She asked me to hold it to the light and read the inner surface. Becoming a Baggins, I read aloud, "Todd, you are my density. Love, Trissa."

I was overwhelmed. The line was inspired by our favorite line of dialogue from *Back to the Future.* George McFly became my hero.

~ "a self-assured tornado" ~

OUR QUICK honeymoon to downtown Seattle (we saw the musical *Cats*) fading into the past, our move into a house in Covington complete (with a bank account soon-to-be-drained by a leaky roof), and Kinski with her boa replaced by a seascape painted by Trissa's Auntie Elsie, we settled into married life.

Trissa bravely went along with my first filmmaking project in four years. I'd carefully worked it out, spending two hours writing while lying on the beach. She played a character based on David Bowie's stranded alien from *The Man Who Fell to Earth*, but when the special effects proved daunting (my script described a spaceship landing), her character became a drifter who shape-shifts from our black cat Mookie. (No special effects were necessary. When Mookie closed his eyes, I cut to Trissa opening hers.)

Paul played a bum who has his heart shattered when his precious wine bottle slips out of his arms and smashes on the ground. Rob acted the short but pivotal role of a drug dealer who has stashed cocaine in a child's yellow plastic Flintstones lunchbox. (His one shot remains my favorite. He became his character, wearing an overcoat, and the way I walked with the camera in one direction while he walked toward a car in the other looked cool. I became Martin Scorsese.) Trissa's cousin La Rue portrayed a drug mule and gave a comic performance. He can do this wonky thing with his mouth, raising his lips on one side while lowering them on the other. I asked him to look at the camera while driving and do it. He complied and didn't crash. Marilyn brought to life the bit part of a woman who is lost and driving about Seattle. She appears to tail La Rue, causing him to panic and ditch the lunchbox in an alley before speeding away.

Paul finds the lunchbox and carries it around for a while but leaves it behind while mourning his wine bottle. Trissa wanders by and takes possession of the lunchbox. After eating a nasturtium (her moment of improv; she assured me the flower was edible), she gives the lunchbox to a boy, Jay. He opens it, gives his goofy interpretation of my requested look of disgust, and pours the white powder into the gutter before heading home with the empty lunchbox. His sister, Molly, washes the cocaine (powdered sugar) away while rinsing our soapy red Corolla.

The movie expressed my fascination with choices and branching—computer programming again. The lunchbox connected the vignettes as it passed from one character to the next. IF the drug mule hadn't become frightened and tossed the lunchbox out his car window, IF the bum hadn't broken his wine bottle and forgotten about the lunchbox, IF the drifter hadn't wandered by and found the lunchbox, or IF the boy had been curious about the taste of the white powder, THEN the cocaine might have found a victim instead of being harmlessly added to the sewer system of the city.

I conceived the movie, *Lunchbox*, as my version of Richard Linklater's *Slacker*, a movie with an easily distracted camera, always glancing away from characters to never look back, instead following someone else for a while. Linklater delivers an opening monologue in a taxicab about how the mere thought of Dorothy and the Scarecrow in *The Wizard of Oz* taking the other road created separate realities.

Where would I be if I'd gone to school in San Diego? Where would I be (or not be) if Monica had said yes? This idea fascinates me, but it can escalate in a hurry. If you branch twenty steps of events happening one of two ways, you calculate 1,048,576 different ways your life could have gone. (If you don't believe me, Google "wheat and chessboard problem" sometime.) I'll keep it manageable and be happy Monica said, "Why are you doing this?" And Trissa held out her left hand.

As a teenager, I loopily avoided talking to girls until my IF condition (aided by Mom's urging) switched to TRUE, and I asked LeeAnne to join me for a movie. During my young adult years in Seattle, I once again dated women the wrong way until I "crashed" as if my dating life had a coding error, a bug. THEN Aunt Gwen's words nudged me down the path of communicating the real me.

"You have to talk to them to get to know them," Aunt Gwen had said. (I doubt she meant one day writing a personal ad.)

Words and experiences of all three of my life's formative women—Aunt Gwen, Cheryl, and Mom—helped me pick the letter on the right side of my coffee table, the big final IF of this whole dating thing.

When Dad left us, I had a decision to make—follow him or follow Mom. At the time, I told Cheryl I wanted to live with Dad, a notion unbelievable to me now, but Dad has gone through de-evolution in my mind over the years. While the females of my life have all evolved into vital present-day species, Dad has fared poorly. Selective pressures have threatened his existence. Once my hero—as most dads are to most sons—he's become, shall I say, the dodo of my life's story—extinct and flightless. (I looked up dodos to make sure they were indeed flightless and successfully verified my fact. I also learned that the birds are thought to have made up for this deficiency by being fleet of foot. They were adept at bravely running away.) Dad always had a thing for butterflies, but my parting image of him shuffling in and out of his fifth-wheel camper twenty-five miles outside of Mandan and barking at his two granddaughters to remove their shoes before entering, characterize him as far more dodo than monarch in every sense of the words. I'm sure he eventually found himself in Monterey, but far from fluttering.

Cheryl gave me a bewildered look when I said I had wanted to follow Dad. She's a storyteller. She knows the possibilities inherent in *that* potential version of her brother. She was another female two years younger but ages older than me. Her expression reminds me of the biggest IF statement of my life. I *was* the Scarecrow and I had to choose between two roads. One followed Dad into a story with an ending I'll never know (involving condominiums) but a reality all the same because I thought (and am thinking) about it. The other followed three women of my life along a road leading to an Emerald City and an ending I never would have imagined for myself as a teen, one conceivably written by Barbara Cartland, Janet Dailey, or, yes, Cheryl.

AN EARLY reader of this book commented: "That Trissa. She came into your life and blew you away like a self-assured tornado."

I mentioned the comment to her, and she laughed. "I'm not self-assured at all," she said.

"Well, it's all relative. Compared to me, you are."

While going to high school, she felt every bit as insecure as I did. She never went to any school dances and had one boyfriend who stuck around Williston and one "boyfriend" who moved to Florida. When I ask her about the latter, she responds with a silent grimace.

But how did she, a North Dakota gal, come to be living in Seattle with her sister and soon to be brother-in-law? When I asked her to refresh my memory of this story, she said, "Are you sure? It's a whole book all by itself."

Still living at home in Williston after finishing college in Minot, she sat, as I had, and tried to figure out what to do with her life. She had a teaching degree and wanted to do something with kids.

She met a guy in a bar, a real smooth-talker and Williston oil field worker. Randy. She gave him her phone number and he called her the same night.

"I don't remember what we talked about, but we talked for hours," she tells me. "I was so impressed by him calling me right away instead of leaving me hanging. I thought it meant he was really into me."

"So, you were falling crazy in love?" I asked.

"Yeah, that's one way to put it. We dated for two months and then he lost his oil field job. He packed and moved back to Los Angeles and wanted me to go with him. I told him no but kept thinking about it. I thought it would kind of fizzle but after he got back to LA—well, Irvine actually—he started calling me every night."

After a few phone calls, she mentioned her quandary to her parents, expecting them to talk sense into her. Instead, they didn't care. They said, "It's *your* life."

After calling Randy, she hopped into her yellow Chevette and hit the road. He claimed he couldn't wait for her to arrive.

She planned to live with Randy forever. "But I quickly learned he was a chaser," she said. "Once he'd caught me, the excitement was over, and he was out of there. Instead of spending my life with him, I was suddenly in a huge city, all alone."

With Randy no longer in the picture, she had zero interest in Los Angeles and started driving to Seattle where her two sisters, Marilyn and Gail; aunties and uncle, Ruth, Grace, and Bill; and Cousin Kim lived. She headed toward family but wasn't ready to head back home to North Dakota—not yet.

As she approached Redding, she heard her brakes squealing and, instead of risking the mountainous driving ahead, she pulled into a garage to have them do whatever they needed to do to make them stop squealing. She took a walk about the town for a few hours and returned to pay the damage and hit the road again to learn they'd checked with her bank, found her account balance lacking, and done nothing.

"I tearfully called my dad. He talked with the mechanic, made sure I had money in my account, and got the repairs underway. Another hour of walking about the town of Redding and I was finally back on the road."

(While we were engaged, her Chevette died for keeps. Without hesitation, I took her to an Avis rental car sale and bought her a Red Corolla. It made me feel chivalrous, not to mention filled with car nostalgia.)

"Funny thing about that drive to Seattle is I don't remember ever spending a night in a motel. Did I drive the whole way without stopping other than spending a stupid bunch of hours walking around Redding?" she said.

Upon arrival, she moved in with Marilyn and Rob to save money. And she might've been hanging out with them from then on, waiting for me to enter the picture. (Who knows? In this alternative reality, she may not have responded to any personal ads during our one crucial week.) But no, her life took another turn.

She found a job through a nanny service. She'd be living with a wealthy couple—no baby yet—a pretty, young, and pregnant wife with her older husband. "It was your typical trophy wife kind of thing," she says. The plan was to live with them in Eatonville, Washington, move to Aspen, Colorado for the birth, and spend time vacationing in Marseille, France. Or, rather, Trissa would be confined to an apartment with a baby while the couple frolicked in France.

It played out…differently.

The couple had a dramatic fight after an old girlfriend phoned him. The wife threw his prized possession address book into the fireplace as he watched horrified. In the morning, Trissa found half-burned pages all over the living room floor he'd tried to rescue. The wife flew to Aspen without him. He hopped a plane the same day to kiss and make up. He told Trissa to drive his pickup to Aspen, leaving her Chevette behind in Eatonville.

Kissing worked, the baby arrived, and calm returned. The husband was a New Agey guy who was into holistic medicine, an occupation attractive to celebrities. Trissa met Buddy Hackett and Barbi Benton and says they were sweet. She spoke to Diane Ladd on the phone. "Honey, can you take down a message please? … Oh, thank you so much, you're a sweetheart," Ladd said. (That's the closest Trissa's ever been to David Lynch's *Wild at Heart.*)

Their house thrived as a crazy place with people coming and going. A channeler flew in at one point to hold a séance. For half price, the woman looked deep into Trissa's soul and informed her she'd been a Native American woman named Grey Eagle and had known the baby in a past life. One of the no-shows on the guest list for the evening: Goldie Hawn.

Another houseguest fell on the ski slopes to be rescued by Jack Nicholson. Or, at least, that's the yarn he spun for anyone who would listen.

Trissa has no idea why, but the couple decided to hire a second nanny. They had one baby. Was it an Aspen version of keeping up with the Joneses?

"I have three nannies. How many do you have?"

"Just one."

"Dear! How do you ever manage?"

The new nanny, also from the Washington State agency, was older, more seasoned. After a week, she took Trissa aside.

"These people are awful!" she said. "We gotta get out of here!"

They hatched a great escape plan. No tunnels were dug. They clandestinely acquired tickets for a red-eye, called a taxi, and split, not telling their employers until it was too late for them to do anything about it. (During the planning, they talked to the couple's secretary in Eatonville. She told them, "Make sure to order the taxi, wait for it to arrive, and *then* tell them you're leaving.") Upon landing in Portland, Oregon, the elder nanny drove Trissa back to Eatonville, wished her well, and Trissa hopped into her Chevette.

And back to Seattle she drove. After Trissa settled into their spare bedroom, Rob and Marilyn referred her to the family of an architect: four young kids, my *Lunchbox* actors Jay and Molly—along with Andy and older sister Megan. Andy and Jay were the *Young and the Restless* babies.

Their house, where she worked when I met her, stood off the shore of Lake Washington and four houses away from Kurt Cobain and Courtney Love and their child's house. Neither of us ever spotted them.

She exaggerated by saying the story had enough material for a book (she just smiled at me and said she'll keep talking if I'll keep typing), but it's packed full of plenty of ways for her to have not been in Seattle for me to meet her (255 other possible realities by my quick estimation). In various alternate universes, I suppose, we might have met in scary Los Angeles or at the Cannes Film Festival.

Trissa lived in Seattle, ready to find a man to put an end to her own dating thing, and beyond ready to marry and have kids. I lived near Seattle, and in the same frame of mind. Our lives had aligned. What a stroke of luck! The week (or rather second week) I decided to run my ad, she decided to step into a photo booth and answer a few.

LUNCHBOX PREMIERED in our living room to raves and, same as with my earlier filmmaking spurt, I quickly wrote another script. Unfortunately, I attempted to become too cinematically sophisticated. I borrowed back the Beaulieu camera from the coworker who had taken it off my hands and toyed with slow-motion—again. I shot both black-and-white and color footage with the idea of intercutting the two for psychological effect. I filmed an elaborate sequence with Paul strolling about a nearby neighborhood with a cardboard box over his head. And I could go on, but there's no point. It was a mess.

The shoot did include, though, what I consider to be *the* moment where my two loves intersected and became one. I was bemoaning the lack of a way to shoot a tracking shot of Marilyn walking toward our house for a key scene.

"Wait a sec," Trissa said before disappearing into our backyard. A few minutes later, she reappeared pushing our beat-up wheelbarrow.

"Hop aboard," she said.

Take after take, she happily pushed me the length of our driveway as I strove for the perfect shot. To her credit, it was the one *nearly* perfect shot in the whole movie.

While shooting a beach scene for that follow-up effort, fated to be abandoned and tossed into a drawer with my *Psycho* footage, Trissa cradled her baby niece, Emily, in her arms. A week later, after three years of trying, including countless occasions of her reaching for the Tampax in tears as I sat next to her trying to conjure something consoling to say, Trissa became pregnant—like magic.

~ hee hee hoo ~

THE PREGNANCY went by without a hitch, almost. A few days before the due date, a cat screech emanated from our garage. We looked at each other. We both thought the other had let Al Lee Kat back inside. I ran toward the sound. I could hear a distressed *meow*. I followed it to the open door of the clothes dryer. I looked inside. Al Lee Kat was lying among the white load of underwear, socks, towels, and sheets with blood streaming from his head. My eyes followed a trail of blood from the dryer, along the floor, and onto a table where an empty cardboard box had fallen from the rafters. On the table, I saw a saw blade with blood dripping.

I drove frantically to an all-night emergency vet. We arrived and were in luck. Al Lee Kat and I had the place all to ourselves. Trissa couldn't go inside. She remained in the car, shaking.

"My cat is dying!" I said.

"I wish you'd called ahead," the oddly distracted receptionist replied.

She glanced at his bloody mess of a head, shockingly unconcerned. She told me to take a seat. I protested. My cat needed help right away. He was bleeding profusely, and it was my fault for not letting him in from the garage. Then reality arrived.

A car squealed into the parking lot and a man, out of his mind, came running in carrying "an animal." All I could tell for sure was the thing in his arms had fur and enough blood to sate a jaded connoisseur of Herschell Gordon Lewis (the gory horror movie director of *Blood Feast*). A vet came running out from an exam room to meet him.

"What caliber gun?" the vet asked.

"I didn't know it was loaded," the man answered.

The examining room door slammed behind them.

Al Lee Kat and I sat alone with our misery in the waiting room. I peered into the pet taxi. He looked dazed, but the bleeding had stopped. His expression said, *What's going on, Daddy?*

Eventually, an assistant came out and took us into an examining room. She shook, but held herself together, barely. She cleaned Al Lee Kat, a vet stopped in and took a quick look, handed me a bottle of liquid pain medication, I paid, and we left. Trissa went into labor the next night.

We stumbled into the hospital well before dawn. There wasn't a soul on the streets or in the hospital lobby. I ran to the front desk and rang the bell while Trissa trailed behind.

"I'm in—My wife's in labor!"

They ushered us into a room, and we had the entire bleary-eyed staff at our disposal. A nurse asked a few quick questions, took vital signs, and told us to go home.

"You're kidding?!" I said.

"Okay. I'm sorry. I'm sorry," Trissa said.

Before leaving, she needed to use the bathroom. After a few minutes, she yelled, "Todd, call a nurse!"

When the nurse arrived, she poked her head into the bathroom and looked at me and said, "I guess you guys are staying after all."

I peeked in and Trissa stood in a puddle of amniotic fluid with more still flowing down her legs.

Left alone in the birthing room, Trissa wanted to relax by taking a shower. I then realized why she'd told me to bring my swim trunks. Within minutes, we stood in the shower, her naked, me semi-nude, and imagining how embarrassed I'd be if a nurse walked in on us.

"Push on my back…yes, right there," she kept telling me and I pushed and pushed.

We'd attended birthing classes and I'd taken notes. To this day, I still have the cheat sheet I pulled out of my pocket whenever I panicked:

- *Deep cleansing breaths*
- *Hee Hee Hoo*
- *Pant (to keep from pushing)*
- *Change positions frequently*
- *Get up and walk*
- *Go to bathroom every hour*
- *No drug decisions during a contraction*

She moved to the bed, was monitored, had her cervix measured, and was told, "Not yet, it's too soon for an epidural."

"Okay, okay," Trissa said. Each time they left the room, she said, "Todd, it hurts so damn much, make them give me something."

I was out of my element. I'd read the books and I had my notes, but nothing told me what to do when my mild-mannered wife screamed, "I don't care what you do. Just make them give me an epidural!"

"*Hee hee hoo. Hee hee hoo,*" she kept saying as the contractions peaked. Each time, I took her hand and joined the chorus. At one point, she stopped *hee-hee-hooing.* She'd briefly lost consciousness. *Come back! I can't do this parenting thing alone!*

After an eternity, the doctor came in, stuck his fingers in her and said, "We can do it now."

Relieved, Trissa cried. As they rolled her on her side, she farted.

"Excuse me," she said, touchingly polite, given the situation.

A doctor whipped out a needle the size of a stinger on a prehistoric mosquito and plunged it straight into her spine. I cringed and bent over, the closest I came during the whole experience to passing out. Her tears changed from relief for the needle to fear of the needle to pain from the needle. After they finished puncturing her, taping tubes into place, and propping her head with pillows, I noticed her tears had stopped. She laughed.

"Oh my God, this is good stuff," she said.

The doctor told us nature would take its course and it would be about an hour of contractions before we'd be welcoming our daughter into the world.

With Trissa happily watching television, I asked if I could take a short walk and find something to drink, as if the "get up and walk" in my notes meant me.

"Okay, honey," she said.

She would've said "Okay, honey" if I'd suggested we move to Thailand, and she hates the tropics. I wandered off. I intended to walk to the nearby cafeteria and buy a Coke, but found it closed. So, I kept walking through a tunnel to an open cafeteria at the far end of the hospital, deliberated between regular, cherry, and diet, settled on regular, and walked back, yawning all the way. I returned to a room filled with people and activity, Trissa frantic. I'd lost track of time, like when I step into the shower at 6:15 a.m. with something on my mind, reawaken when the water turns cold, and emerge from the bathroom to discover it's 6:57 a.m. and I'm late for work.

She was being told to push…and the birth happened so quickly I didn't realize it had happened. I heard cries and saw Amanda in the doctor's hands. It's all else a blur except for two vivid memories.

"Would you like to cut the cord?" a nurse asked while thrusting scissors toward me as if it wasn't a question at all. I now think of Anna Karina snipping the air in Godard's *Pierrot le Fou.*

I took the scissors and tried and tried, but found the cord impossible to cut. I'd always imagined it would have the texture of sausage. Instead, it was a garden hose. The nurse had to help me.

And a different nurse asked, "Do you want to hold your daughter?"

Trembling, I said, "Yes."

In slow motion, I took Amanda into my arms. I know she couldn't focus on anything yet, but I swear she stared into my eyes for hours.

Baby Emily's charms had kick-started Trissa's ovaries, but

shouldn't they have remained happy? It would again take three years of trying and crying to conceive Rachel, who was born by cesarean section in Bismarck, North Dakota—the gruesome details of which I have no memory because I wouldn't look beyond the surgical curtain. Once again, I have two vivid post-birth memories. I couldn't hold her right away. Nurses whisked her off to an incubator and later that day all we could do—me standing and Trissa seated in a wheelchair—was watch her cry through a window. Another memory worried me for days. While Trissa was splayed open, the doctor poked around and found a growth and sent it to the lab. Did she have cancer? No, it turned out to be a freaky cyst that, according to the doctor, had hair and teeth. We declined to keep it in a jar for posterity.

While trying for baby number three—the one we agreed to have while walking and talking around Capitol Hill on our first date—we decided to check the mood of my testicles. All our infertility efforts had been focused on fixing the mommy wannabe. Well, it turned out my millions of tiny men didn't march either. (Or they were the sole culprits all along.) My sperm, with their scant count, sluggish motility, and whatnot lazed about and boxer shorts failed to motivate them.

I had a morning appointment to drop off my sample. I'd read the instructions. I knew keeping it at the right temperature and placing it under a microscope as quickly as possible was essential for proving my manhood, but the logistics seemed impossible unless I jumped into my already running car and drove maniacally. So, I decided to play it safe and do my thing at the clinic.

I settled into a bathroom stall. I had the men's room all to myself. I took out the plastic cup and unscrewed the lid. I placed both in my boxers, bunched up around my ankles. I tossed my head back, closed my eyes, and conjured whatever arousing images I could. (Too embarrassed, I didn't have assistive literature rolled under my arm.) I heard the men's room door open, and someone walked in, stepped into the stall beside me, and stood there, not peeing or anything. He groaned and belched. It broke the mood entirely.

"*Goddamnit! Arrgh! Uuugh!*" he uttered, not knowing or caring he had an audience.

After many minutes of concentration, I dribbled over the finish line, screwed the lid in place, regained my composure, and pulled my pants back up. The guy still belched away as I left.

I had to walk about fifty feet from the men's room to the counter to hand my sample over to a lab assistant. I gave her my name. She pulled my chart. I handed her the cup. She looked at it. She looked at me.

"There's not much in there, is there?" she said.

WRAPPED IN the sentiments of remembering how I fell in love, I told a lie a few pages back. Trissa and I *have* had one fight. It didn't last long. No blood. Five angry words spoken, all by her. Okay, it was one-sided—her angry, me apologetic. It wasn't a fight, and I didn't lie after all.

I'll set the scene. It was our first night home with Amanda. We felt exhausted. I had neglected for weeks to replace the bulb in the kitchen ceiling light and we thus had a flickering table lamp on the counter by the sink. Trissa sat in bed holding our baby, frustrated. She'd imagined throughout her pregnancy the joys of breastfeeding, but Amanda was having none of it. She refused to latch on. Oh, and I, as they say, had one job.

We'd had bottle supplies on the kitchen table for weeks. The bottles had a plastic bag. You fold the bag over the bottle, fill it up, and screw on the cap. I was supposed to practice this and master this and had done neither. I did it for the first time with the pressure on in the semi-darkness. Amanda screamed from hunger. Trissa yelled at me to hurry. I tried to adjust the water to the right temperature and measure the formula powder correctly. I stirred it and poured it into the bag and screwed on the cap and ran to the bedroom. Trissa took the bottle and expertly guided it toward Amanda's mouth, but the top, which I'd inexpertly failed to tighten, fell off the bottle and doused both with formula.

"Damn it, Todd! Hold her!"

I took Amanda in my arms. Trissa went to the kitchen to make a proper bottle. I followed. I kept quiet, afraid to say anything. Halfway through the preparation, she bumped the lamp with her elbow, and it flickered one last time and went out. She finished making the bottle in the dark, took Amanda under her arm, and headed straight back to the bedroom, kicking the door shut behind her.

Learning how to make bottles and fixing our kitchen light became my top priorities in life.

"I'm sorry. I'm sorry," I said at every opportunity. How was I ever going to make it up to her?

Five months later, at work on a Saturday, my desk phone lit up. It was Trissa.

"Todd," she said, sounding weak, crying.

"What's wrong?"

"I'm…I think…I think I may be having a stroke!"

"Do you want me to call 911 or head home?"

"Home—"

I floored it. When I pulled in front of our house, an ambulance was blocking the driveway. I rushed inside as they rolled Trissa out the front door on a gurney.

"Are you her husband?" a paramedic holding Amanda in his arms asked.

"Yes."

He handed Amanda to me. We hopped into Trissa's car with the car seat and tailgated the ambulance all the way to the hospital. *I know nothing about children. I can't do this without her!* I thought. (Trissa remembers me as oddly calm during this episode. She was worried by how calm I looked. Truth was, I was a wreck.)

We sat in the waiting area while doctors evaluated her. A nurse walked us into the examining room where the love of my life dressed, put on her shoes, and held her head.

"It hurts so much," she said.

"What's wrong?"

"A migraine probably brought on post-pregnancy. I never imagined they'd be this painful."

We slowly walked to the car. I had to hold her up. She carried a plastic garbage bag.

"What's in the bag?" I asked.

"Nothing, yet," she said.

Yet? I wondered. After driving for a few minutes, I knew. I heard her gag in the back seat, then vomit flowed—a geyser. I didn't know a human could vomit so spectacularly. I thought of characters in *The Exorcist* or *Stand by Me*. It was merely the beginning.

The rest of the day, she became buddies with a bucket. I became handy at carrying said bucket back and forth between her and the toilet.

After two days, the headache waned. We relaxed. *That was horrible*, we thought, *but it's finally over*. A day later, the pain returned—and the vomit. For a week, the cycles of pain and throwing up alternating with hopeful respites continued. We visited the doctor. He did nothing but prescribe stronger pain pills. They didn't help.

Realizing I had missed a lot of work and we couldn't see any light at the end of the tunnel, we called Trissa's mother, Phyllis, in North Dakota and asked her to fly in to play nurse. Two days later, I gathered her at the airport.

The migraines continued to perform their terrible play for her eyes. After two iterations, Phyllis became convinced the vomit contained blood.

"I think it's the tomato soup you gave her," I said.

"No, it's blood!!!"

The next time Trissa puked into the bucket, Phyllis stopped me on my trip to the toilet. She scooped vomit out of the bucket with a Dixie Cup and poured it into a ziplock bag.

"What are you doing?!" I asked.

"We're going to the doctor. Now! And I'm taking this. They need to examine it for blood."

An hour later found us sitting in a waiting room. I held Amanda. Phyllis clutched a bag of puke. Trissa sat between us, looking ghastly, half because of her illness, half because of her mom. When the nurse arrived to take Trissa into the examining room, Phyllis handed her the vomit baggie.

"See, there's blood right there, I know it," Phyllis told the nurse while pointing at a speck of red floating amid chunks of corn and bits of saltine cracker in phlegm-filled water.

The nurse took it daintily between her thumb and index finger, trying in vain to hide her disgust. Obviously, the baggie wasn't going anywhere near a microscope.

The doctor prescribed a drug called a beta blocker. It did the trick. The terrible cycles ended. Better still, Phyllis boarded a plane and flew back to North Dakota.

(That story came out of my keyboard sounding like stereotypical mother-in-law stuff. I *did* appreciate her being with us during those trying times. She provided comfort to Trissa and Amanda enjoyed having her grandma around. Phyllis did the cooking—mostly tomato soup—and I returned to work. But it's another one of those situations where the memories I kept were mostly troubling.)

Something similarly disgusting happened months later. Trissa and I were enjoying a date night. We'd dropped Amanda off with Marilyn and Rob and Cousin Emily, had a nice dinner out, and caught the movie *Orlando* at the Egyptian Theater. We arrived back at their house to retrieve the kid and head home. The front door was locked. I knocked. The door opened. We could hear the wailing of two girls in the background.

"You're gonna love this," Rob said, waving us inside.

Marilyn and two hysterical girls huddled on the kitchen floor. Rob paced back and forth, waiting.

"We suspect they got into a box of rat poison. I talked with poison control. I've already administered syrup of ipecac," he said calmly.

Trissa added herself to the huddle. The reality dawned on me. And soon two tiny bodies convulsed, heaved, sobbed, and sought the laps of their mommies for comfort, over and over.

Seeing and hearing Amanda's inconsolable crying reminded me of the time we attended Seafair. We camped on the beach for the flyovers by the Blue Angels. Every time the planes roared overhead, Amanda's tears escalated, and she demanded to be in the arms of whichever one of us wasn't holding her. Back and forth she went. But her body convulsing under the effects of ipecac frightened her far more than jet aircraft. Only the comfort of Mommy would do. I stood and watched.

Serious as Sherlock Holmes, Rob dropped to his hands and knees, soaking the legs of his trousers in the vomit, and with his face inches from the floor, wiped in circular motions searching for tiny green granules. I hunkered beside him. I couldn't bring myself to join him in his finger painting, but I wasn't grossed out. Fascinated, I kept my eyes peeled for bits of poison as well. We never found any. By midnight, both girls were, and their moms mostly were, back to normal.

Getting married was a journey. Having children has been an adventure. There was nothing perfect about our first tiny house, nor any house we've had since. The only things idyllic about our paradise: two girls—each in turn dragging my childhood blanket behind her—and our love for each other.

I emit a deep sigh of relief because I share my life with Trissa. I know Monica and I wouldn't have survived the turn my marriage took next.

Two years later, Rachel was born in Bismarck and we settled into our new life.

~our travels began~

WHEN I was a kid, Dad's den always seemed mysteriously well stocked. He had more pencils and pens than a human could possibly need in a lifetime—and the pile grew by the day.

He'd often sneak in through the garage carrying brown grocery bags, but instead of continuing toward the kitchen, he'd swing a hard left and head for his desk, closing the door behind him. He'd emerge a few minutes later, folding the bags and notice me watching.

"Don't you have homework to do?" he'd ask and then he'd point toward his den. "See that room? That's my home office. Keep out!"

Something about those times stuck with me. Plenty of Initech issued pens, pencils, pencil sharpeners, and, at one point, a fresh box of typewriter ribbon found their way to my car. (I *was* a screenwriter after all and needed to keep my typewriter in good working order.)

Why am I confessing this?

Reading film festival programs all day at my desk and movie-harassing Charity were whiffs at a fastball and a slider leaving me trembling in the box, about to be "let go" by Initech. Swiping office supplies caught the outside corner of the plate. (I wonder what mistakes Dad made to be "let go" by IBM.)

My boss Bob's boss—also named Bob (so many Bobs)—followed me out the door one day while I was carrying a ream of typing paper. (Shades of getting drunk and trying to bicycle away with an entire box of punch cards.)

He caught up with me and placed a hand on my shoulder. "Todd, do you like working here?"

Missing the point of his question entirely, I thought, *He has no idea.* I could never tell Mom I hated being an engineer. She'd paid for my education. I'd made a beeline for a diploma without once questioning if I wanted it. (People who go to college are too young to go to college, I've since decided.)

He held out his hand and I finally caught his drift. I handed him the paper. His arm dropped six inches from the sudden added weight.

"Have you ever taken anything else?" he asked.

"Um, no. Well, I did swipe your red stapler last week," I replied—again forgetting why lies were invented.

His face lit up.

I was dragged into Human Resources a few weeks later—on a Friday—and told I'd soon be laid off. I would be on the streets in two months and had two options—cash as a going away present or an all-expenses-paid training course in small business planning. After contemplating taking a copy machine out into a nearby field and smashing it with a baseball bat, I chose the latter. (And by now—if not long before—you've probably realized the *Office Space* game I've been playing with Initech.)

I decided to become a magazine publisher. Desktop publishing was the craze. I found a book at the library about it and everything. *I can do* that. *It looks easy*, I thought.

"You can give it a try, but it has to be in Mandan," Trissa said.

I proposed creating a magazine about arts and crafts. My business plan, as written, had a small chance of success, but it was a lie. I wanted to try to become a radical, leftist zine editor and movie critic. The magazine I planned to create, *The Open Forum*, would've been at home in Paris, France in the late 1950s with Jean-Luc Godard, François Truffaut, and Eric Rohmer darting about, but not North Dakota during the Clinton years.

I briefly flirted with one other idea during those transitional months. One of my Initech coworkers was friends with a Hollywood film editor—one of the guy's biggest credits at the time: 2nd Assistant Sound Editor for *The Abyss*. I wrote him a letter asking for advice about moving to Los Angeles (a place still scary to me, proving the depths of my desperation) to look for film editing work. He wrote back and asked me to call him.

"Do you have any schooling or experience?" he asked.

"I've cut some Super 8 on my kitchen table," I said.

"Are you married? Do you have kids?"

"Yes. One little girl."

"You don't want to do this," he said. "It's hard enough for guys who went to film school and are young and don't have any ties. I lived in my car and ate beans out of a can for my first year."

We small-talked a bit more and I hung up—dejected *and* relieved. Narrowly avoided images of Steve Martin at the end of *The Jerk*, clutching a thermos and sleeping in an alley stinking to high heaven flashed through my mind.

Soon after, the wheels turned. The house had sold. We had an apartment lined up in Mandan. Trissa gave notice at her nanny job and we sold (including, unforgivably, my teenage record collection) or tossed everything we couldn't cram into a modest Ryder Truck.

As our move approached, I made frequent trips to Seattle to watch artsy movies. For my final trip, I saw Mike Leigh's *Naked*. Trissa thought about again trusting Amanda to Marilyn, Rob, and Emily and accompanying me, but this one had "naked" as its title.

I visited my favorite bookstore, Cinema Books, one last time and spied two curious volumes: *Hitchcock's Films Revisited* and *Hollywood from Vietnam to Reagan*, both by a guy named Robin Wood.

"I warn you. Those books are difficult," the bookstore owner, Stephanie Ogle, told me.

Two days later, I kissed Trissa goodbye and hopped into the truck with Amanda and our travels began. We climbed mountains and traversed open plains. Every time I filled the gas tank, she cried in her car seat until I returned, fearing she'd been abandoned. Trissa followed us to North Dakota a week later with her sister Gail, Al Lee Kat, and our newest cat Bee Bop (Gail kept Mookie) in her Corolla because she'd committed to one final nanny gig with Andy, Jay, Molly, and Megan.

While driving, I looked at Amanda and thought about

Trissa. *Hitchcock's Films Revisited* perched atop the diaper bag waiting to be cracked open.

"That's all I need," I said to Amanda.

As Dad had been when "let go" by IBM, I was okay with Initech kicking me to the curb. I didn't enjoy working there. I wanted *something* else. Those three strikes against me may not have been what I would have chosen, but they pushed me toward somewhere else.

in·er·tia

a property of matter by which it continues in its existing state of rest or uniform motion in a straight line unless that state is changed by an external force.

Two years later, Rachel was born in Bismarck and we settled into our new life. I remember times sitting on the couch with Trissa's legs upon my lap, Rachel rolling about on the floor, and Amanda pacing back and forth in front of the television holding her light blue, stuffed gnome doll, Pippin. Watching *Rugrats*, she'd laugh at the mechanical cat teetering about and at how Tommy Pickles squirts formula from his bottle into his parents' faces. Was she remembering my first attempt at bottle preparation?

~"please call me Arnie"~

BEFORE MOVING our lives from Seattle to Mandan, we vacationed in Santa Barbara. At church, while helping Mom welcome people at the door, I shook my third grade teacher's hand. Ms. Pigeon. She'd always been my favorite teacher and another formative woman in my life. I told her I feared living in North Dakota.

She smiled and said, "Todd. I've known you for a long time and one thing I know about you is you'll find a way to be happy no matter where you are."

I recall nodding my head and smiling. I didn't believe her, but her words stuck around, and I thought about them for days. I didn't have any counter evidence. I am, generally, a happy person.

I consider it one of my life's most pleasant surprises: After spending my youth in the land of silent era Hollywood premieres, where I regularly visited the Arlington Theater, and passing a decade in film-obsessed Seattle, I found my greatest cinema bliss in Bismarck/Mandan.

When Trissa said I could create a magazine, but it had to be in Mandan, I protested. (Okay, I whined.) She must've spoken with her brother, Dean, who lived in Bismarck and told him about my existential crisis, because about a week before hitting the road I opened a letter from him. Well, not a letter, but an envelope containing a newspaper clipping—a *Bismarck Tribune* story about a film series hosted by Bismarck/Mandan's local film organization, The Cinema 100 Film Society. Seeing *Farewell My Concubine*, *Indochine*, and *Wise Blood* on the list of offerings excited me. I hadn't seen any of them yet. Dismayed, I noticed the series would end a week before I would arrive. Still, it offered hope. I also noted the president of the organization had included his name, Arnold Lahren, and phone number at the bottom of the article.

During my first evening in Mandan, after tucking Amanda into bed, I sat at our new kitchen table, still cluttered with unopened moving boxes, and dialed Arnold's number. Nervous, I could feel sweat soak through my T-shirt. *This guy's a president of a film society. Should I be bothering him?* I wondered. After two rings, a deep voice, comforting and calm, answered.

"Hi, I'm calling for Arnold Lahren."

"Speaking."

"I have this newspaper clipping about the Cinema 100 Film Society. I just moved to town and love film and was hoping I could get involved with your society in some way," I pleaded my case.

"What's your name and number?"

"Todd," I said. (I also gave him my number, of course, but I don't remember what it was. It's been a while. Besides, if I published it and people called it, who knows who would pick up?)

"I got you down. I'll be sure to include you in our next meeting. Just be sure to come with a long list of films you want us to bring to town and a hearty appetite. John Halloran hosts the meetings and he's a great cook."

"Thank you."

"Anything else I can do for you?"

"I don't think so."

I started to say goodbye when he said, "Oh, Todd. One more thing."

"What's that?"

"Please call me Arnie."

Our brief phone conversation initiated my, so far, twenty-seven-year relationship with the organization. The life-long friendships I've developed have made me feel right at home. They're as passionate about cinema as everyone I met through the Seattle International Film Festival.

One of them, Brian Palecek, is an arts lover of many colors. He's a fan of James Joyce who makes a celebration of Bloomsday an annual affair and who reads, enjoys, and understands (or claims to comprehend) *Finnegans Wake*. He's a classical music buff who gives introductory lectures before Bismarck/Mandan Symphony performances and has a life's goal of seeing performances of every opera ever composed. My favorite experience with Brian came during the days when he programmed the calendar for the defunct One World Coffee House in downtown Bismarck. He allowed me to program a cult film series for Saturday nights. I screened *Monty Python and the Holy Grail*, *Akira*, and *Female Trouble*.

Time passed and before I knew it my phone rang. The meeting to plan the 1995 film series had arrived. Arnie reminded me to bring a hearty appetite.

"John is near world-renowned for his bread and soup."

Arnie had warmth and an easygoing, laughing nature about him. I relaxed in his presence. A Bismarck State College English professor with a talent for bonding with young people (I was thirty-two—not young), he treated me as if I'd been attending these meetings all the way back to the organization's origins twenty years prior. He—and everyone else—valued my newbie wish list as highly as ones brought to the table by longtime members. I didn't have to fight to be heard.

I still have a copy of Arnie's notes, written in his flowing cursive. The two movies I most wanted to include—the indie favorite *Spanking the Monkey* and the last movie I'd seen in Seattle, Mike Leigh's *Naked*—were included. I chuckle as I look over the list we created. Along with being accommodating, Arnie knew how to scratch his own itches. He'd inked in *Sunset Boulevard* and *Elmer Gantry*.

After each Cinema 100 screening, people would gather at a restaurant—the Hong Kong or the Rockin' 50s Café—to discuss the film we'd shared. Whichever restaurant we chose, we always secured the largest table—and often had to slide several tables together. Arnie always sat at the head of the table(s), leading the talk, lending a careful ear, and taking notes.

He considered those discussions an essential part of the experience. We'd always drive home afterward with an enhanced appreciation for the film, but he had loftier goals than our enlightenment. He wanted to be prepared to lead the discussion the following day with the students in his "Film as Literature" class. Students were required to buy a series ticket, see all the movies, discuss them in class, and write about them. Those students, Upper Midwest still-teenagers, often felt challenged by the movies and would sit in class ruffled and rattled. Arnie knew how to handle the situation and turn it around—and this is my favorite anecdote about him. He insisted the students speak their minds, but also say at least one positive thing about the film. By the end of an Arnie-led class, ill feelings became buried beneath an avalanche of positivity.

In 2002, *Apocalypse Now Redux* found its way into our series. It's an often-hallucinogenic journey along a river during the Vietnam War. I'd long been a fan, but this re-edited version was new to me. It contains sequences Francis Ford Coppola had removed in 1979 during a mad editing frenzy—and severe loss of confidence—to ready it for the Cannes Film Festival. The two standouts: a long scene with Playboy bunnies inside a grounded helicopter and an encounter with members of a lost-in-time French colony. Since I was reading the writings of Carl Jung at the time, those two additions captured my fancy. After the screening, Arnie and I walked out to our cars together. (No dining was planned because the film had been lengthy, and people wanted to head home.)

"Lots of people don't like the French plantation sequence," I said.

"Oh, why's that?" Arnie asked. "I loved it."

"They think it grinds the movie to a halt, but I think it's super important. One of the things about all the male characters in the movie is they're out of touch with their female side, that anima thing Jung wrote about, and one by one they all do a horrible job of breaking up with their wives. I think what Willard learns in the movie is how to contact his feminine side."

"Interesting," Arnie said.

"But the original cut misses the point. It bungles it. This version shows the guys interacting with the bunnies instead of just ogling them from a distance. That was great, but the French plantation really brings out the theme. Remember what's blaring out of the helicopter speakers during the attack on the village?"

"Wagner. 'Ride of the Valkyries,'" he answered.

"Yes! I've always loved that scene, but it made the movie feel front-heavy as if something is missing during the second half. Valkyries are goddesses who descend from the heavens to rescue worthy soldiers from the field of battle. And that's what happens, visually, during the added scenes. The beautiful Aurore Clément invites Willard, the one officer who hasn't sent his wife a brutal 'Dear Jane' letter, upstairs to her heavenly bedroom to reward him with a night of pleasure. It's the payoff to his whole story."

Arnie listened to my impromptu babble (most of which I still agree with) and commented, "You and Jung are onto something."

What makes me smile about this episode is how he listened to my off-the-cuff film analysis, jotting mental notes for the following day's class discussion, while ignoring the conditions: five degrees below zero with a blizzard underway and his car door two feet away.

I have difficulty remembering when it happened or what year. I could look it up but knowing would hardly matter. I arrived in the lobby of the Grand Theatres to see the first film of our latest series and noted something amiss. My fellow board members weren't smiling. They appeared devastated. I approached Brian Palecek.

"What's wrong, Brian?"

"It's Arnie. He was diagnosed with brain cancer. Terminal," he said, his voice choking up.

Along with everyone else, I sat on one of the lobby's padded benches and tried to wrap my mind around those words. I must've gone into the theater and watched the film, whatever it was.

Arnie occasionally, bravely, attended screenings, supported by his wife, Lynn.

When time arrived to plan another season, Arnie gathered

us at the Unitarian Universalist Fellowship & Church of Bismarck-Mandan. He was hanging in there, but weak. He opened the meeting with his characteristic smile but cried as he made his announcement. He would have to resign as the organization's president. We all took turns comforting him, but he urged us back toward the agenda.

"I'll be okay. We have work to do," he said.

I had been laid off (again—which I guess makes this 2004) and Arnie knew it. Once his brief display of tears subsided, he had two concerns for the remainder of the meeting: twelve great titles for our series and my well-being.

At the time, Arnie and Lynn lived north of Bismarck near Washburn. I kept putting off making the drive to visit them. *It's such a long way away and I still have time*, I reasoned, in deep denial. I didn't know how to deal with the situation. I'd never met dying and death before. Nothing fills me as deeply with guilt as the phone call from Brian telling me Arnie had passed—and I had never visited.

I attended his memorial service at Bismarck State College, unable to accept the truth. I didn't shed a single tear as speakers referred to him as everything from a true renaissance man to the heart and soul of Cinema 100 to the kindest person they'd ever known.

To me he was and is still alive.

Arnie loved Marilyn Monroe. His estate donated his sizeable collection of photos of the movie star to the Grand Theatres, where it hangs on the wall leading from the old wing toward the new addition. I always pause to admire the photos when I visit, and I often return home thinking about Marilyn. My favorite of her roles is *Some Like It Hot*. Arnie preferred *The Misfits*. I never asked him what he thought of Theresa Russell's portrayal of her in *Insignificance*, where she explains the theory of relativity to Albert Einstein, but I'm sure Arnie—always fond of the famous photo of Monroe reading James Joyce's *Ulysses*—enjoyed it.

A year later, I browsed through boxes of books at the annual Bismarck Memorial Public Library used book sale when I came across one waiting just for me. It held cinema-related books: *The Celluloid Closet*, *Kubrick Directs*, and *How to Read a Film*. I plucked them from the sale box and placed them in my items-to-be-purchased box. At one point, I opened one for a bit of browsing and saw the words: "Property of Arnold Lahren" inked in his unforgettable cursive.

My tears arrived.

CINEMA 100 friendships aided me in my first big endeavor in my new home. Arnie and Brian wrote columns for my dream project. The newspaper I created, *The Open Forum*, didn't become the radical zine straight out of late 1950s Paris, France I'd envisioned. It morphed into a home for all the mostly left-leaning, artistic types in town to express themselves. It had essays, short stories, poetry, and a few cartoons. It had artwork by my greatest of all discoveries, Jonathan Twingley. I had grabbed a cup of tea at the Green Earth Café and noticed a box of postcards for sale. I adored them. I bought one and called the artist. I remember being nervous and sweaty once again. The voice of a personable high school boy answered. I told him about my paper and asked if he'd help.

"Sounds great. It'd be my pleasure," he said.

He contributed artwork, essays, short stories, an excerpt from an illustrated novel, and his spirit to all fifteen issues. I adore his illustration for my review of *Pulp Fiction*. He's since moved to New York City. I still follow his work.

I created *The Open Forum* to become a film critic in the hardest way possible. Retyping submissions sent to me through the mail, trying (and failing) to sell ads, learning page layout, working with the printer (same press as *The Finder* and *The Mandan News*), and replenishing free stacks all over town in the dead of winter in a used Subaru without a working heater (my car had become unsexy) was exhausting. All that work erected an elaborate contraption with one purpose—delivering my movie review to the world each month. (Similarly, this memoir is a construction designed to hold a single confession. It was easier to be a self-styled movie critic a few years later when the Internet became a thing.) My first attempt at becoming a neo-Roger Ebert: a review of *Forrest Gump*. Rereading it, I notice my fascination with a feather floating out of the sky, choosing Forrest seated on a bus stop bench to be the story's hero for a while, before blowing away again. "Life is like a box of chocolates" indeed.

I had a blast writing for *The Open Forum*, but I eventually ran out of money and had to seek real jobs again. I self-taught my way into web programming and database design—and, thus, found a way in North Dakota to satisfy my near lifelong interest in programming as well. (How else did you think I knew about JavaScripting?) But I'd caught the film reviewing bug. I've been a film critic on the side ever since. I wrote reviews for a few small publications—*River's Edge* and *The Prairie Independent*—and then *The Bismarck Tribune* held a contest. "Write and send in a movie review and we'll reward the winner each week by running it in the paper," the rules stated. I flipped to the movie theater ads, chose *Juno*, headed out to the theater to give it a watch, and started typing:

> *There are times when the critic in me finds himself totally disarmed. Some movies accumulate such a mountain of little pleasures that they dare me to burrow in and look for flaws or to even attempt analysis. I'll find myself sitting in the theater with a smile from start to finish and overwhelmed by the feeling that (almost) everything is perfect.* Juno *is one of those movies…*

My review won. (Who knows? They may have only received one entry.) I chatted with the editor, one thing led to another, and I found myself with a weekly gig. My eighty favorite reviews I wrote for the paper over the next couple of years are included in my book *See You in the Dark*.

My best reviews had a way of tapping into my personal life. One of my favorites shows me still grappling with memories of my summer with Monica. (I'll admit I changed her name to the protagonist in my favorite Ingmar Bergman movie, *Summer with Monika.*)

> Blue Valentine *is an achingly sad affair. It chronicles the final days of a marriage between Dean (Ryan Gosling) and Cindy (Michelle Williams), seemingly held together only by a young daughter (hers, not his) and desperation (his, not hers) …*
>
> *What went wrong? The answer he finds is pretty much everything. But it's a very understandable sort of everything, or at least it was for me. In my twenties, I fell in love at first sight and ignored all the signals the pretty young woman was flashing before my eyes until we found ourselves sitting before a roaring fire enacting "the marriage proposal scene." The woman, hand trembling, gave back the ring, stood up, and walked out of my life.*
>
> *I was lucky. I was spared what I now know would have been years of sadness…*

Trissa starred in a review, after I once again proved my non-talent for selecting date movies:

> Knocked Up. *Hmm, I think a better title would have been Snuck Up because this baby snuck up on me twice…*
>
> *I finally got around to seeing it with my wife and was pleasantly surprised. I loved every minute of it. From start to finish, I was either smiling or laughing or nodding my head with recognition of the characters' plight. I found it wonderfully observed. It wasn't a stupid sex comedy about getting laid. It was a stupid sex comedy about getting laid with a heart, one that cared about and understood its characters much like the first* American Pie, *another film that snuck up on me.*
>
> *Driving home, the film snuck up on me for the second time. My wife said, "That was a complete dick flick." I cleaned the wax from my ears and asked her to say it again. She said, "That's a movie only a guy could love." I thought to myself, "That's a new one. A film containing pregnancy tests, birthing classes, women sitting in bed eating*

> *ice cream, and a child delivery scene full of knowing details ('I need an epidural now!!!') seemed to me to be chick flick city. How could this be a dick flick?"*
>
> *Reading back now over what I just wrote, those are all things I know from my direct experience with the whole having babies thing. Those are all things any guy with kids should know. They are all having-a-baby clichés. Maybe I overestimated the quality of observation because I was having such a good time…*

I've found cinema-happiness living in Mandan. It surprised the heck out of me, but not Ms. Pigeon.

My third-grade teacher knew me well.

OOPS!

As if she had a looking glass and foresaw my future scuba diving near-drowning, she feared my going near the surf.

WHILE VACATIONING at a cabin at Hume Lake, I took a hike. I was around ten years old. Off I went, not telling anybody. It was a wonderful day. The sun already felt warm, birds sang, a deer and her doe scurried away as I approached, and I'd made a quick slice of toast on my way out the door. I was ready for anything—a true explorer.

I followed a creek upstream into the mountains. How far? I don't know, but I eventually felt hot. I took my sweatshirt off and tied it around my waist. I crossed the creek and wandered along the opposite side. I worked my way over to the dam, tossed a few rocks into the water, noticed hardly any boats still on the lake, and followed the rapidly flowing runoff into the unknown. At one point, I decided to cross the rapids for the sake of crossing and stood contemplating the four-foot leap and the wet, slippery, mossy rocks. I took note of the rapids awaiting me if I slipped. I jumped.

When you're young, death doesn't enter your moment-to-moment calculations. I made it across the rapids at Hume Lake. I didn't die. Hours later, I wished I had.

I followed the stream for a while until it hit me—hunger. I looked about, paying attention to my surroundings for the first time, and noticed the sky darkening. I knew I needed to hurry, or I might not have enough light to see my way back to the cabin. I'd spent the entire day wandering, daydreaming, tossing rocks about, and tempting death. It was time for my weary explorer to hike back to the cabin and eat. Keep in mind, it was wild country. Bears lurked about, not to mention mountain men, and the worst came out around dusk. Our garbage cans had been bear-raided the evening before.

As I climbed the final hill to the cabin, something about the picture appeared off. Ranger trucks parked askew and a bunch of strangers in uniforms stood on the cabin's huge back deck. I stepped onto the far end of the deck, silently as always, and watched. Everyone faced away from me, circled around the picnic table. I observed, fascinated, realizing what I saw was unfolding in my honor. I would've related with Tom Sawyer returning home to observe his own funeral if I'd taken Aunt Gwen's advice and read it. One of the rangers turned, saw me, and stepped aside. I saw Mom and Gramma Dirty sitting at the table distraught and embracing. They both saw me at the same instant. Gramma Dirty jumped to her feet, raced toward me, and I flinched as she grabbed me.

"Where were you? Why did you do this?" she shouted.

"I don't know. I don't know," I replied.

Screaming and crying ensued. Mom remained paralyzed.

AS A teenager, I drove around town with Cheryl doing some shopping when I stopped at a red light. I turned up the radio and the car started shaking. I turned the knob back, but the shaking worsened. Being a novice driver, I still had a lot to learn about the workings and behavior of automobiles. (I'm still clueless.)

Oh my God, I thought, *I've overheated it and we're going to die in a ball of flames!*

I turned off the engine and dammit—the shaking continued.

I've really done it. The car is so overheated it's going to explode when it isn't running.

I looked at the stoplights and they were bouncing. I peered at people in cars around us as Guido does during the opening of Fellini's *8 ½* and they all gazed back at me with fear in their eyes. How had I screwed up the car so badly I'd affected the whole world?

Cheryl gasped, "It's an earthquake!"

From then on, we sat back and enjoyed the show. People raced out of stores and ran amok in parking lots. I relaxed—and why not? We were in the safest place we could be, in a car where nothing could fall on us. The movie *2012*, with images of the earth opening wide to swallow cities, awaited far in my future.

When the shaking stopped, I flowed along with the cautious traffic. We decided what the heck, we may as well continue shopping while gazing upon the destruction all about us as if arranged for our amusement. It wasn't long, though, before we realized our plans for the day would have to be scrapped. Stores have a way of closing for the day when all their merchandise has tumbled from the shelves and is piled in the aisles.

We had experienced the epic Santa Barbara quake of August 13, 1978. (Yeah, a year Dad still wore polyester. What a summer that was.) On a sunny Sunday afternoon, the earth shifted abruptly underneath the channel causing an M 5.2 earthquake. The initial rupture started on an offshore fault, south of the city, at a depth of about 5.5 miles. It ruptured northwestward, focusing its energy toward nearby Goleta. One-third of the books at the UCSB library—400,000 volumes—were thrown to the floor, a landslide blocked San Marcos Pass, and a freight train passing through derailed by a kink in the tracks. The town would spend weeks restoring to normal. I worked as a warehouse man for a paper goods supplier and soon learned I'd be spending one of my last days of the summer restacking paper towels and toilet paper.

Without shopping to do, we took the scenic route home and well over an hour after the quake we turned the corner into our cul-de-sac and came into view of our house. People had gathered in our driveway, which irritated me because I had to park in the street. We walked toward the mob and the crowd parted to reveal Mom, sobbing, comforted by neighbors. When she saw us, she had an outburst of anger, relief, fear, happiness, sadness, and exhaustion.

The neighbors' gazes surgically dissected me, trying to discover how I could be so thoughtless.

I'VE FOUND countless ways to cause Mom worry. I should've withheld this next story from her. It's from well into my North Dakota-living days:

I'm not certain which I heard initially: the crinkling of a Lay's Cheddar & Sour Cream potato chips bag or the pounding of tires against center median warning bumps. I watched our van drifting off I-94 west of Dickinson at 79 mph. I was sitting in the back with Rachel beside me. She startled from her Game Boy. Trissa occupied the front passenger seat and Amanda, still clutching her learner's permit, held the wheel with one hand, trying to free her other hand from the potato chips bag.

The cruise control stayed engaged (why did we allow a learner to use cruise control?) and Amanda faced numerous challenges and too little experience to calmly tap the brake and nudge the steering wheel. In a panic, instead, she pulled the wheel to the right with all her might. We changed direction instantaneously ninety degrees and cut straight across the freeway toward the right shoulder.

In a letter to the editor of *The Bismarck Tribune*, I likened what followed to the wildest roller-coaster ride ever designed. I rolled upside down, sideways, and traveled backward, all of it surreal as if time had come to a standstill. Then all *was* still. The van rested on its crushed roof, engine still running, drive wheels still spinning. Amanda instinctively turned off the engine fearing we would soon explode. She's *almost* always been one to calmly keep her head. The gist of my letter to the editor: we survived thanks to us all wearing seat belts.

I released my seat belt and checked on everyone.

"Are you okay, Rachel?"

"Yes, Dad."

Amanda had already wiggled free from her constraints as I crawled along the roof toward the front of the van, disoriented. Why was Trissa calling for me from the left side? She hadn't been driving.

"Todd. Help me!" she pleaded.

Her head was bleeding. Everything from luggage to iced tea bottles to compact discs had flown everywhere. We never knew for sure what had sliced into her forehead. She hung from her seat belt, unable to find the release. I pressed it for her and caught her as she fell.

We all emerged through the shattered side windows and collapsed in the late winter snow. I hopped to my feet and re-checked everybody. Amanda sat, leaning forward with hands on her head, sobbing.

"It's okay, Amanda. We're okay," I said.

Rachel sat mesmerized and watched her mom's blood flow as if in a dream. I noticed voices. People had surrounded us. Vehicles moving in both directions had stopped and Good Samaritans had rushed to our aid.

Strange coats were wrapped around shoulders by unseen hands (we discovered we still had one of the garments a week later). A bare-chested man attended to Trissa's head with a T-shirt. Another young man, bearded, twenty-five, asked her how many people had been in the van.

"Four," she answered.

Two young women ran toward the van and searched the wreckage. I continued to walk back and forth.

It slowly dawned on me their desperate search was for me. I'd forgotten all about myself. I felt fine. I knew I wasn't injured. My family was my concern and, thus, I didn't appear to our saviors as one involved in the accident. The fear in their voices said they were trying to locate a body.

During my next Sunday evening phone call with Mom, I told her what had happened. She became quiet for a long time. When she finally said something, she sounded as if she'd been choking and told me not to worry.

"I took a sip of my drink and it went down the wrong tube," she said.

Obviously, she'd been crying. In the same way I'd entered her world, I'd almost left it in an instant of "Oops!"

...Sadly, because it took me so long to write this, the second promised book, my mom never had a chance to read it, or any version of it.

I'm writing this letter during the time of COVID-19 in 2020/21. One of the characters in my story, Jenny, nearly died from the virus. (I named her after one of my favorite movie characters, the girl/woman who's always there for Forrest Gump.) She was hospitalized for weeks and became one of the first people to receive compassionate application of the drug Remdesivir. Within a few days, she began to recover. She was one of the many people in this story I had wandered away from. Once I'd found your mom, I no longer needed her help with hookups with single ladies. Repeatedly, it's come as an undeserved surprise to me she's stayed in touch. She called me and offered her condolences when Stanley Kubrick died. When your grandma died, she sent me a photo of her grandkids impatiently watching cookies bake in the oven—cookies made by following your grandma's recipe. And when she fought COVID-19, she included me in her private ICU messages about her condition. Like Paul staying my friend after I ditched him, she's remained my friend for 35 years and counting.

Don't do as I did. Keep your friends close.

The monologue in Paris, Texas *where Travis reconnects with his estranged wife, Jane, captivated me back in 1984. It didn't move me, though, and I now use it as a way of gauging how much I've changed. As I experience that scene and watch Nastassja Kinski's slowly shifting expression, I barely even hear his words as I wipe away tears. I guess it's natural. So many people have entered—and left—my life—so many monologues I wish Sam Shepard had written for me.*

Just thinking about the movie makes me want to curl up and watch it again with both of you.

I love you,
Dad

~the movies~

In order of first appearance, the movies referenced in this memoir:

Always (1989)
The Dark Knight (2008)
The Wizard of Oz (1939)
2001: A Space Odyssey (1968)
Star Wars (1977)
Monty Python and the Holy Grail (1975)
The Shining (1980)
Saturday Night Fever (1977)
Dazed and Confused (1993)
The Song Remains the Same (1976)
Dawn of the Dead (1978)
Back to the Future (1985)
Fast Times at Ridgemont High (1982)
Return of the Jedi (1983)
The Force Awakens (2015)
The Last Jedi (2017)
Octopussy (1983)
Moonraker (1979)
1941 (1979)
Close Encounters of the Third Kind (1977)
Kramer vs. Kramer (1979)
All That Jazz (1979)
Ordinary People (1980)
The Grapes of Wrath (1940)
Forrest Gump (1994)
Detour (1945)
Jaws (1975)
The Deer Hunter (1978)
Coming Home (1978)

Cutter's Way (1981)
The Jerk (1979)
2 or 3 Things I Know About Her (1967)
Easy A (2010)
A Clockwork Orange (1971)
Superman (1978)
The Searchers (1956)
Rashomon (1950)
Citizen Kane (1941)
Willy Wonka and the Chocolate Factory (1971)
E.T.: The Extra-Terrestrial (1982)
Dressed to Kill (1980)
Blow Out (1981)
The Discreet Charm of the Bourgeoisie (1972)
Pink Floyd: Live at Pompeii (1972)
Night of the Living Dead (1968)
All of Me (1984)
Taxi Driver (1976)
And the Ship Sails On (1983)
The Graduate (1967)
Office Space (1999)
The Fellowship of the Ring (2001)
Amadeus (1984)
Paris, Texas (1984)
Rosemary's Baby (1968)
Boyhood (2014)
Dune (1984)
Dune (2021)
Stranger Than Paradise (1984)
Cry-Baby (1990)
Who Framed Roger Rabbit (1988)
A Hard Day's Night (1964)
Young Frankenstein (1974)
Gardens of Stone (1987)
Ghost World (2001)
Madame Sousatzka (1988)
Little Shop of Horrors (1986)

Blue Velvet (1986)
Dead Men Don't Wear Plaid (1982)
Zabriskie Point (1970)
Psycho (1960)
The King of Comedy (1982)
Joker (2019)
My Life as a Dog (1985)
Street Trash (1987)
8 ½ (1963)
Vagabond (1985)
Black Panthers (1968)
Wings of Desire (1987)
Apocalypse Now (1979)
What's Opera Doc? (1957)
Vertigo (1958)
Barfly (1987)
Annie Hall (1977)
Fight Club (1999)
Full Metal Jacket (1987)
The Last Temptation of Christ (1988)
Slacker (1990)
The Fabulous Baker Boys (1989)
Rear Window (1954)
Polyester (1981)
Nashville (1975)
Crossing Delancey (1988)
Portrait of a Lady on Fire (2019)
The Grandmother (1970)
Eraserhead (1977)
Wild at Heart (1990)
Raising Arizona (1987)
Planes, Trains and Automobiles (1987)
Parenthood (1989)
The Naked Gun (1988)
The Man Who Fell to Earth (1976)
The Great Escape (1963)
Blood Feast (1963)

Pierrot le Fou (1965)
The Exorcist (1973)
Stand by Me (1986)
Orlando (1992)
The Abyss (1989)
Naked (1993)
Farewell My Concubine (1993)
Indochine (1992)
Wise Blood (1979)
Akira (1988)
Female Trouble (1974)
Spanking the Monkey (1994)
Sunset Boulevard (1950)
Elmer Gantry (1960)
Apocalypse Now Redux (2001)
Some Like It Hot (1959)
The Misfits (1961)
Insignificance (1985)
Pulp Fiction (1994)
Juno (2007)
Summer with Monika (1953)
Blue Valentine (2010)
Knocked Up (2007)
The 40-Year-Old Virgin (2005)
American Pie (1999)
2012 (2009)

~about the author~

Todd Ford leads two lives. By day, he's a systems analyst for a utilities company. By night, he's a reader, writer, movie lover, and guy on a mission to combine all three. He lives in an empty nest with his wife, Trissa, in Mandan, ND. Together, they've had twelve cats and two dogs.

Made in the USA
Middletown, DE
20 April 2022